HOLY HOLLY

one tiny life

4-6-2024

Dear Laura,
It is such a joy to share my memoir with you! Enjoy!
Love, Debra Nelson Holm

A MEMOIR *of* FAMILY
LOSS *and* RENEWAL

HOLY HOLLY
one tiny life

DEBRA NELSON HOLM

SAVORING FRUIT PRESS, 2022

Holy Holly: One Tiny Life is a work of creative nonfiction. Some names and details have been changed to protect the identities of persons involved. Photos were taken by family members and are used with permission. Forty percent of the profits from this book will be dedicated to the farm fund of the F. Wayne and Joyce Furniss Nelson Living Trust.

For information about discounts and orders by trade bookstores, wholesalers, book clubs, film options, or translation rights, please contact the publisher.

Holy Holly: One Tiny Life

Published by Savoring Fruit Press /Debra Holm Writing Services

Nampa, ID USA

Published 2022.

First printing 2022.

Printed in the United States of America.

ISBN 978-1-7320247-2-4 – Holy Holly: One Tiny Life print version

ISBN 978-1-7320247-3-1 – Holy Holly: One Tiny Life e-book

DEDICATION

This book is dedicated to sweet Holly, to my parents, and to the parents, families, and caregivers of health-compromised children everywhere. Your sacrifices are beacons and gifts to those around you, including the siblings of ill children.

I sing praises to a loving God who helps us learn the meaning of love and sacrifice.

Preface

Sharing a simple story is complicated.

I unintentionally wounded my mother's heart when I started this project in 2007. As we read my five-year diary together, she shrank from the casual way that twelve-year-old Debbie had scribbled about all aspects of our lives at the same time Mama was fighting for Holly's life. Mama couldn't bear the thought of anyone exposing her personal Gethsemane to the world. Sensing that God had a timetable we couldn't see, I set the story aside. Mama died in 2009.

When Dr. Ronald K. Lechelt discovered letters about Holly in his desk in 2016, and against all odds, found our family and sent them to us, it was an unexpected miracle. We were thrilled, and I dug into the job of combining diary, letters, documents, and family memories into a book. Then I stopped. I dug in again. And stopped.

Time and time again, our family's painful story stalled. Eventually, I had to face a hidden psychological barrier—my inner child, blocking me with fears like those Mama had felt. I asked this hurting child to allow me to write our truth and promised her that we would both be okay. She consented. God pulled me back into His rhythm, and this book is the result.

Living people permitted the use of their names, except that a few students' names and identifying details were changed to protect their privacy, and some doctors' names were abbreviated to protect their privacy. I'm grateful to Dr. Lechelt, Dr. George Veasy, and Mr. Gerald Gee, my sixth-grade teacher, for fascinating and helpful insights granted in interviews.

While every aspect of actions, conversations, and scenes may not be factual, they are as authentic as I can make them. Other people may interpret events differently. I refer to Teton City, Idaho, as "Teton." That's what we called our town.

Acknowledgments

To my husband, Norman Holm: Thank you for emotional and financial support and for helping when I shouted, "This computer is wonky!" I'm deeply thankful to Patricia Bess, my artist friend, and sounding board—always optimistic, always encouraging; and to Olivia Herrell, my ever-patient writing buddy—an honest critique-er, an excellent writer, and a formatting and self-publishing guru who shares time and talents generously. As I spilled my heart through many drafts, these dear ones, along with my family members, lifted me.

To my siblings, Judy, Bruce, Ellen, Jeanne, Brenda, Rex, Andrea, and Shanan; to my cousin, Marilyn, and your families: thank you for living this story! Thank you for your perspectives, memories, and photos. Events presented here may not line up with your recollections—

they don't fit entirely with mine. We're more complex than the parts we played in this saga, and to capture the essence of any one of us in a few words is futile. Thank you for allowing me to share our family's story with the world.

I send love to beta readers: my siblings, daughter Lara Holm Roetto, Olivia Herrell, and Marilyn Marshall. I thank Lara, Olivia, and September Fawkes for critiques on early drafts and my daughters Emily Holm Murdock and Alissa Holm Aldous for arduous final editing work.

I sincerely appreciate Jennifer Stimson for creating inspired cover and interior designs. She made Holly's story shine! She was endlessly patient with my constant changes.

I thank the good people who lived in Teton and Clementsville, Idaho, in 1967—what beautiful places to grow up!

Most of all, I thank my Savior Jesus Christ, who supported me and kept the vision of this book in my heart, and sweet Holly Joyce, my mother, and my father, who taught me the meaning of love purified by sacrifice.

TABLE OF CONTENTS

Introduction

I met Holly the night before my twelfth birthday.

"Time for bed!" Dad said, turning off the TV. My brother and sisters scooted, but Mama placed my hand on her tummy. Something moved! Something small but firm arced an orbit under the skin of her belly!

"It's our baby," Mama whispered. "He—or she—is growing there, safe and warm, right under my heart—where you grew twelve years ago."

Wow—that bump on Mama's belly was a baby?

My world in the small town of Teton, City, Idaho, (we shortened it to "Teton") was about to change. My unborn sister—Holly—would shape my life and the lives of my entire family profoundly. At school I was tormented by students who looked down on kids from the dry farms. Especially me: the meanest and baddest bully targeted *me*, and I thought that was torture.

But it was nothing compared to watching my baby sister struggle to survive day in and day out while my family, especially Mama and Dad, fought to care for Holly with incredible tenderness and a lot of prayer.

Every minute of our time with Holly taught us lessons in love.

Let me tell you the rest.

In loving memory of Holly Joyce Nelson,

Debra Nelson Holm

Four photos show the Wayne and Joyce Nelson family as we were prior to Holly's birth, and two photos show the homes where we lived.

Joyce's pregnancy with Holly had just begun when this photo was taken. From left to right: Rex, Wayne (Dad), Alan Jeppesen, Jeanne Nelson Jeppesen, Joyce (Mama) with Andrea in front, Debbie (me) with Shanan in front, and Brenda. Photograph taken in Alan's parents' home in Boise, Idaho, in August of 1966. The birth order of Wayne and Joyce's children was Judy, Bruce, Ellen, Jeanne, Brenda, Rex, Debbie, Andrea, Shanan, and later, Holly.

Silverio "Silver" Hidalgo and Judy Nelson were married in June of 1963. This photo was taken at their reception in the Teton building of The Church of Jesus Christ of Latter-day Saints. Their son Michael was born in 1964, and they lived in Fort Hall, Idaho, in 1967.

Bruce Nelson was stationed in Grenoble, France, with the United States Army in 1967.

Kerry Frazier and Ellen Nelson were married in November of 1965 in the Idaho Falls Temple of the Church of Jesus Christ of Latter-day Saints. They lived in Rexburg, Idaho, in 1967.

We rented this pioneer-era stone house in Teton from 1956 to the 1990s, when Judy Nelson Scoble purchased it from heirs of the Briggs family. The window on the right is the "girls' room," and the window on the left is the living room. Six tall Norway spruce trees stand in front of the house. Prior to 1968, we lived here for most of each school year and at our dry farm in the summer. The one-room schoolhouse near the dry farm closed in 1954, necessitating the move to town for children to attend school. Many fathers also took winter jobs in town to supplement their farm income. Starting in 1968, we lived in this home year-round. This 2020 photo is courtesy of Kara Hidalgo. Daniel and Kara Hidalgo have lived in the home for many years.

The Nelson farmhouse in 2010. It was re-sided in the 2000s. To those who say, "You had two houses? You must have been rich!" we reply that we only had enough money to get by. After Dad and Mama sold the farmland and kept the home in 1965, we moved to the farmhouse during the summer because we loved living among aspen and sagebrush. We kept a cow and a pig in the barn and pastureland, we grew a garden (located where the people are on the right side of this photo), and Dad and the boys had a shop where they could weld and repair equipment for their work spraying pine trees in the forests. Our family paid the taxes over the years, and we continue to camp here every summer.

Prologue

Monday, February 6, 1967

TETON, IDAHO

I'd felt Mama's baby move. I wondered, *Is this baby a boy or a girl? A boy would make Dad and Mama happy after seven girls and would send my brothers into outer space with joy. I hoped for a girl. The world needs more girls. Take my sixth-grade class: nineteen boys and only four girls.*

"When, Mama?" I murmured.

"Around Easter. We've never had a baby born then, when all the world is new and we celebrate the resurrection of Jesus Christ." Mama pulled me closer. At forty-six, a little gray salted her dark brown hair. Lately, bluish half circles sagged under her eyes, and she rested on the couch more than usual. A feeling pinged in my stomach—a vague idea that something was not right. I pushed it away. Mama's spirit was as vibrant and optimistic as a twenty-year-old. Nothing could be wrong.

Even as my jealous heart whispered, *Just what this family needs: another person to pull Mama away from me*, she held me tight and smiled into my eyes. At that moment, I was the only person in her universe.

As I crawled between chilly sheets, shivering with excitement and the cold of an Idaho winter, I thought about the people in Mama's orbit. She—Joyce Furniss Nelson—made a lot of people feel good about themselves. They included my Dad, Wayne Nelson, age fifty, and my eight siblings. This winter, Dad was working at a potato warehouse. He'd been a farmer and a prospector, and now, most of the year, he was a "bugger." (That's a person who sprays trees to kill pine beetles—"bugs.")

Dad and Mama's oldest child, Judy, twenty-five, and her husband, Silverio "Silver" Hidalgo, were parents of three-year-old Michael, the first grandchild—my nephew! Judy was a registered nurse who compassionately bandaged all our injuries, and Silver had finished a stint in the United States Army. They leased a farm in Fort Hall, Idaho, where they lived.

Bruce, twenty-three, served in the U.S. Army in Grenoble, France, though he yearned to be with his buddies in Vietnam—in the middle of battle. Mama was thankful he wasn't in 'Nam.

Ellen, twenty-one, and her husband, Kerry Frazier,

lived near us in Rexburg, Idaho. Ellen straightened our collars and smoothed our hair, blessing us with her innate sense of style. Kerry could wallop any decent softball pitch into a homerun and catch any ball that flew near shortstop.

Jeanne, twenty, had married Alan Jeppesen the summer before. When they drove off to the University of Idaho in Moscow, Idaho, a piece of my heart went with them. Jeanne was unfailingly kind to everybody. She studied home economics and Alan studied English, with a plan to be a lawyer like his father.

Brenda, sixteen, a junior at South Fremont High School, had earned her driver's license and was Mama's preferred errand runner. When I went with her to Rexburg or St. Anthony, the nearest big towns, we dragged Main and she taught me how to scope out teenage boys.

Rex, fourteen, lived outdoors, fishing and hunting. He was building a dune buggy with his best friend. They were in the eighth grade at South Fremont Junior High.

I was almost twelve, a sixth grader at Teton Elementary School. It had been a rough year—none of the girls in my class liked me—but I hoped to find some friends in junior high.

Next was Andrea, seven. When she wasn't reading, she was thinking. Dad said Andrea ran mental circles around her first-grade teacher.

Our baby, Shanan, was a blond two-and-one-half

year-old, a chattering sunbeam who made us laugh. Shanan wouldn't stay our baby for long. A little person was moving inside Mama.

Judy and Ellen were also expecting babies. *How many boys and how many girls will join our family in 1967? I hope it's a sister. I can use any girlfriend I can find, since the other three girls at school hate me.* That thought settled over me like a February cloud as I drifted to sleep.

Mama and Dad relaxing, as they often did, with a newspaper. Mama was frequently too exhausted from caring for her large family to read as much as she would have liked. They both loved the comics and current events, though they didn't always agree on the latter. They loved each other, and their children knew it.

Birthday Disaster

Tuesday, February 7, 1967

TETON

Somebody was mouth-open snoring—either Brenda, Andrea, or Shanan. Not me, but one of us in the girls' room—there were two of us in each double bed, snuggled tight. Wind moaned through the tall pine trees outside, and chilly wisps puffed through frosted windows. I pulled the covers tighter.

The door to the woodstove screeched open in the dining room.

Dad was shoving in kindling, fumbling for a match to start the fire.

Brenda rolled out of bed, turned on the closet light, and shoved through tightly squeezed hangers, looking for an outfit.

"Rise'n shine!" Dad shouted. "Rex, go chop some wood! Debbie, get up!"

I groaned: another day of torture, otherwise known as school. Then I remembered: *No matter what happens, today is going to be fun. It's my birthday.*

It was seven minutes after 7 a.m., and I was officially twelve years old.

"Bye, everybody, happy birthday Deb!" Brenda yelled as she and Rex ran out the door to catch the bus to their schools eight miles away in St. Anthony.

While Mama ironed my skirt, looked for matching socks, and brushed Andrea's hair, Dad cooked. As soon as we were dressed, he placed a plate of thin sourdough hotcakes in front of me. I reached up for a hug—he smelled of bacon grease, coffee, Camel cigarettes, and Lifebuoy soap.

"Happy birthday! We got the best of the deal when I paid the doc who delivered you with stock in that uranium claim."

Dad had raised grain in the rolling hills of Clementsville, Idaho, for twenty-three years after he and Mama married in 1939. During the winters, our family moved from the dry farm to valley towns so the kids could attend school and Dad could work. He did many jobs, including prospecting for lead, copper, and, especially, uranium in the Idaho mountains. That nuclear "hot stuff" was in demand for Cold War research being done at the National Reactor Testing Station in Arco,

Idaho. Dad—and the doctor who accepted 160 shares of "International Lead and Copper" stock in return for delivering me—hoped the claim would pay off big, but it never did. Now Dad sprayed trees to kill pine beetles for the United States Forest Service during the spring and summer, and he found other work the rest of the year.

"Grab your coats, girls, it's time to go!" Mama yelled.

I washed down my hotcakes with milk and headed for the door.

"Have a good birthday, honey," Mama said, giving me a squeeze and a kiss.

"What'll they do for your birthday?" Andrea asked as we trudged down the snow-covered gravel road. Her blue eyes sparkled, and wisps of honey-colored curls escaped her crocheted hat, bouncing against a brown coat that had once been mine.

"Maybe they'll sing. Nothin' special," I mumbled.

"Will your friends give you a present?" Andrea asked. "Jocelyn gave me jacks on my birthday."

"Naah. The girls don't like me, especially Bea."

"Bea's a snot," Andrea said loyally.

"*Andi*, Mama doesn't like you calling people 'snot.'"

"Hey, call me *Andrea*, will ya? Bea is a snot. When I was gettin' a rock out of my shoe, she grabbed my shoe and threw it on the roof of the shed. The janitor had to get it. What about Wendy?"

I sighed. "Wendy hasn't liked me since the first day of school."

"Last year she was your best friend."

"She was. Wendy was my friend from first grade on. We had to be. We're both outsiders, and Bea and Sandy treated us like dirt."

"Outsiders? We live in Teton, like they do."

"Did you know Bea's and Sandy's families were pioneers here in Teton?"

"No, but I know our grandpa and grandma were pioneers in Clementsville!"

"How'd you know that?" I asked.

"You told me when we played pioneers with our dolls and stick rifles last summer. Where's Wendy from?"

"She's from Wilford." Wilford was a small community three miles north of Teton.

"Half the kids at school are from there. Bea's sister in third grade picks on the Wilford kids, too. How come Wendy's mad at you?"

"I dunno. On the first day of sixth grade, I walked in, figuring that Wendy had saved me a seat, but Wendy was with Bea and Sandy in the corner. I stood there, and Bea yelled that I made a better door than window. Everybody laughed, even Wendy. This year, none of them are friends to me." I hadn't told that to anyone but Mama. I sniffed—the frigid air was making my nose and eyes run.

Andrea patted my arm and changed the subject. "Are you taking birthday treats after lunch?"

"Mr. Gee says we're too old for treats." I had told

myself that it was okay, that Mama, tired as she was, shouldn't have to make cupcakes or cookies—the sixth-grade boys would wolf them down while Bea jeered at runny frosting or burnt edges. Another part of me shouted that it was my first year without treats, and I felt sorry for myself.

"That's terrible!" Andrea was shocked. "Mama could bring some anyway!"

"Andi, don't be so stupid. Mr. Gee won't go for that."

"Don't call me Andi!" she yelled, breaking into a run. "I'm not a boy!"

"*Andi! Andi!* You're such a pest!" I shouted.

Bong-dong, Bong-dong, boomed the big school bell.

Better not ruin my birthday by being tardy, I thought as I ran.

Mr. Gerald Gee, sixth-grade teacher and principal over the six grades at Teton Elementary School, walked in as I threw my coat at the hooks on the wall and sunk into my desk, huffing for breath.

Bea, raven-haired and confident, raised her hand.

"Mr. Gee, may I ask Debra something, *privately*?"

He raised an eyebrow. "Quickly, Bea, I need to call the roll."

Bea walked up, leaned over and stage whispered, "The back of your skirt looks like you sat on some cherries. What's *that* mess?"

I'm wearing a bathrobe that my sister made from two bath towels in 1967, with Jeanne's wedding veil and Ellen's gloves as accessories. Over time, I wore this bathrobe into rags.

Birthday Surprises

My period had started. On my birthday!

Mr. Gee called the roll, ignoring the laughter and whispers rippling through the room.

I scrunched down into my seat. *How will I get out of class without everyone seeing the back of my skirt?*

As he called the last few names, Mr. Gee handed me my coat and gestured toward the door. I wrapped it around my waist and sidled out as the sixth grade recited *The Pledge of Allegiance.*

Bea, Sandy, and Wendy looked like little girls, like fourth graders who didn't have their periods yet. Mine had started during the summer. I thought no one in my class knew, but now everyone knew.

I threw open the front door, fell into Mama's arms, and sobbed out my story. "Why is Bea so mean? On my birthday! I can't go back to school, never, ever!"

Mama gently brushed wet tendrils of hair off my forehead. "Twelve years old is old enough to learn: you can't control what other people do—you can only control how you react. Now, go fill the tub; take a soaky bath, but don't get your hair wet."

Mama's solution for every ailment was a long bath in our tub—six feet long—with clawed feet clutching round brass balls. After I had steeped for a few minutes, Mama placed a narrow, contact paper-covered board across the tub and brought in warm, peppery, buttery milk with crisp toast to dip into it. Mama's "soaky bath" immersed me in such soothing grace that I forgot about the sixth grade. I wondered, for the hundredth time, what birthday presents I might get. *Maybe church shoes, since my white flats pinch. A used bike? Pointless, in a foot of snow. Maybe a good book. Or a doll. I might be too old for dolls. Money is tight. I may not get much.*

Mama knocked. "Time to get dressed."

The bath water was cold. I sighed, drained the tub, put on my underwear and robe, and crawled into bed, where Mama found me.

"Mama, I can't go back to school!" I snuggled deeper into the covers, challenging her to budge me. "That would ruin my birthday!"

She smiled. "Are you kidding? Nothing can ruin your 'Lucky Seven Birthday.' Twelve years ago, you were born: our seventh child, born at seven minutes after 7:00 a.m. on the seventh of February, weighing seven pounds and seven ounces. On your seventh birthday, your Great-Uncle Hugh gave you a check for seven dollars and seventy-seven cents!"

She laughed, a little out of breath from the recitation of all my sevens.

"I can't face those kids."

"You can." Something in her voice told me I would go back to school—I just had to come to terms with it.

From Brenda's reject pile on the floor, Mama held up a red wool Stewart plaid pleated skirt that my older sisters had worn and loved, each in their turn.

I sat up. "That skirt fits *me* now?"

"If it's loose, I'll fix it with safety pins." Mama used safety pins and spray starch a lot. They were two of the pillars that supported the Nelson-girl fashion universe. I dug through Brenda's pile, looking for a blouse. In that beautiful skirt, I could face my nastiest enemy.

The class was at recess when I arrived, so I slipped into my seat before they returned. When they came in, nobody noticed me. That was nothing new.

***

My party began when Judy, Silver, and Michael, and Ellen and Kerry arrived. Little Michael's lustrous brown eyes and black hair contrasted with Shanan's blue eyes and blond hair as they raced to find toys. They were the same age and played together more like sister and brother than nephew and aunt.

Ellen showed me a *Seventeen* magazine from the library. "Look at this cute jumper with a curved neckline and armholes, in a floral print. And—"

"He's getting us!" Shanan screamed, as she, Michael, and Andrea ran through the living room, chased by Kerry.

Brenda brought out a cake flaming with candles, and everyone sang "Happy Birthday," with Rex adding his chorus, "You look like a monkey, and you act like one too!" I blew out the candles, and the cake lasted about two minutes.

"Now get busy on those presents!" Dad said.

I hope there's something good in that pile of gifts. I'm not sure what, but something special, something that shows I'm a person who might, someday, have friends.

Ellen and Kerry gave me a blue and green print jumper. "No one will guess I made it from a fabric remnant from the drapery shop where Jeanne works. The rings that connect the shoulder straps to the front of the jumper—they're drapery rings! Try it on!" Ellen said.

In it, I felt as pretty as the *Seventeen* model.

Jeanne had sent me an unusual "robe"—two pink bath towels, sewn together except for arm and neck holes. It was comfortable and weird. I loved it.

"It's different," Mama said. "Anyway, I'm glad my older daughters sew and help to dress you younger girls!"

I opened a pale blue five-year diary from Mama and Dad. It was small but cool. *Imagine writing down some-*

thing on every date, every day, for five years!

Mama handed me a package, and I tore it open to reveal a book: *Hitty: Her First Hundred Years,* Rachel Field's story about a carved wooden doll.

"I loved this book when I read it last year! How'd you get it?"

Mama looked embarrassed. "I couldn't get a copy any other way, so I checked it out from the St. Anthony Library and didn't return it. Then I paid for it."

I leafed through the worn book that I had read before. *Will I take time to read it again? Maybe. We're desperate for reading material, with no library in Teton.* Mama watched me.

"Open the next one; it goes with it."

I tore the paper from a nicely painted, solid wooden box with a hinged cover. Mama and Judy had outlined my initial "D" in fancy brass nails on the lid of the box and had lined the inside with purple satin. A brunette doll, with a few homemade outfits, rested in the box.

"*Your* Hitty doll," Mama said, almost shyly.

I hugged Mama and Judy tightly, sensing the joy they'd felt as they created this gift, listening to them chatter about their work.

Judy said, "This dress matches the satin lining of the box! See, a hoop skirt, like they used to wear!"

A plastic doll? An old wooden box, fixed up? "Thanks, it's neat. Such a great gift," I choked, my insides grumbling with guilt. Mama and Judy had made me a special present, yet here I was, thinking about magical teen-aged gifts Bea had probably gotten for her birthday. I dutifully dressed the doll in a different outfit before Judy and Silver bundled Michael into his snowsuit. Within minutes, the married kids were gone.

Bugging with our packhorse, Cloudy, Dad was ready to spray a diesel solution—a.k.a. "goop"—on lodgepole pines in Idaho forests. Buggers who didn't have a horse worked in teams of two, carrying a spray rod and stirrup pump, which they christened a "grunt pump." The "packers" delivered large cans of goop along lines of trees with packhorses or with our World War II army Jeep.

How We Bug

I hung up my new jumper and put on the robe. I liked them. Bea wouldn't have worn them, but for me, they were wonderful. I put the doll and book in the box and latched it. Mama's face had glowed when she showed me my initial on the lid. "It took a lot of sanding before I could paint it! And the librarian was so nice, not like they usually are when you have to pay for a book."

I might play with the doll—with Andrea and Shanan, sometimes. I might read them parts of the book. If I get bored, I'll re-read it. I traced my finger over the brass D. It wasn't what I hoped for. But Mama and Judy had worked hard.

Next to the box, my new diary lay on the bed. I picked it up. *There isn't much room to tell about all that happens in a day, but that'll make it easier to write a little every night.*

I wrote: ***Tuesday, February 7, 1967: 12 years old. Got this [diary], a new jumper and a towel robe. They really fixed Hitty doll and box. Was lots of fun and I feel great.***

For the next year and a half, I would write in my diary every day.

***

Monday, February 13, 1967

TETON

Rex yelled, "There's not a chair to sit on! So I'm not writing a doggone essay!" He stomped around, running his hands through his curly hair and gesturing at the chairs, which were draped with drying clothes as were two wooden drying racks in the dining and living rooms.

"Quit beefin'," I grunted, glancing up from a book. "Big baby. Grow up!"

"You're one to talk! Always reading. Gimme *your* chair!"

"No! Why should I, you big bully?"

Mama entered, swept damp shirts from the chair next to the desk, and fixed Rex with a steely glance. "Get busy!"

Rex slumped into the chair and chewed on his pencil.

She turned to me. "Deb, put your book down, and roll these shirts for ironing. And help Brenda fold the dry diapers before supper."

Hanging clothes on the clothesline was a year-round job for Brenda and me, but in the winter, they didn't dry—they froze. We brought them into the house to dry. Sometimes Mama ironed the damp out. But tomorrow, that would change.

Brenda pulled her dark hair into a ponytail and picked up a diaper. "Dad, thanks for buying that dryer! I froze my phalanges hanging these clothes at 10 below!"

Dad raised an eyebrow as he shoved chunks of wood into the stove. "Phalanges?"

"Bruce says phalanges is a fancy way to say *fingers*. Where'd you get the dryer?"

"A woman north of town advertised it, said she got a new one for Christmas. With Mama expecting, we need a dryer. But I've got to fix the wiring in the back porch so the thing don't blow a fuse."

We blew a lot of fuses in the gray stone house we rented from Mary Briggs Parker, daughter of George Albert Briggs Sr., who had built this house and the nearby Teton Flour Mill in 1890. At the mill, a torrent of water from the millrace canal poured over a giant mill wheel, turning the gears of large millstones that ground wheat into flour and corn into meal. George Albert Briggs Jr., son of George Sr., or *Bert*, and his wife, Arminda, or *Min*, lived next door to us in a pink brick home with their six sons and one daughter. Bert didn't grind much wheat anymore. He harnessed the waterpower for electricity and sold bulk fertilizer to farmers. Our house was so old that we had push-button switches to turn on the lights.

Brenda pulled Shanan's diapers from a chair. "I don't care if freezing *does* whiten diapers! We'll use the dryer now, and we won't have to worry about the Briggs boys getting a thrill from seeing our bras on the line. It's a drag, hanging towels and sheets on the outside clotheslines and hiding our underwear on the inside lines." Mama protected the world, including the Briggs boys, from the moral corruption that arises from the sight of female underwear.

Rex dotted an "i" and cleared his throat. "Want to hear my masterpiece?"

"Do I have to?" I groaned.

He began: "How to Spray a Bug Tree, by Rex Nelson. Spraying a bug tree can be difficult, dirty, and trying to the beginner..."

"You are difficult, dirty, and trying," Brenda said, winking at me.

Sometimes Brenda and I teased Rex; sometimes it was Rex and me against her. Sometimes they ganged up on me.

"Spraying a bug tree—who *cares*? It stinks!" I declared. Rex scowled.

Mama handed me a stack of plates and shot Brenda

and me a dirty look. "You *should* care—Rocky Mountain pine beetles are killing our forests. The Forest Service pays Daddy to spray trees and kill the beetle larvae, and that puts food in your mouth. Now finish folding those clothes, Brenda, and set the table, Debbie-Dayo."

Counting plates, I thought about my weird family. Mama and Dad were so old-fashioned that they called each other *Mama* and *Daddy* instead of *Wayne* and *Joyce*. And though I hated hearing "beetle larvae" in the same sentence as my "mouth," Mama was right about Dad's bizarre occupation. Dry farming was hit and miss for folks who didn't have large farms. In 1963, Dad and Mama had sold their farm ground to two of Dad's brothers, Lester and Henry Nelson. For the last three years, Dad, along with other contractors, had worked with the U.S. Forest Service to identify and spray affected lodgepole pine trees—a process called "bugging." Dad said government scientists knew they couldn't eliminate all the beetles, but they wanted to slow the spread of the infestation. Dad worked one or two bugging contracts every summer, with his sons and sons-in-law, nephews, and their friends as his bugging crew. *Making a living from beetles is another thing that makes us different from our Teton neighbors who are all potato farmers.*

Rex cleared his throat, gave me a superior look, and continued: "Therefore, I offer a few tips on this occupation. The dirty part you can't get away from, but maybe these tips will make it less trying and difficult. For one tree you will need: a can of bug 'goop,' which is a mixture of diesel and insecticide; a small hand-pump, called a *stirrup pump* by the Forest Service and a *grunt pump* by 'buggers;' a length of hose; and a piece of half inch pipe that is seven to nine feet long with a nozzle on the end, which has also been called a rod, a boom, and a damn nuisance." Brenda and I giggled.

Mama sighed. "Son, remember who'll read it."

Rex scratched the word out and went on: "It's a work-out to walk through the forest carrying a twenty-to-thirty-pound pump with a two-to-three horsepower motor, all attached to a piece of plywood, and twenty-five feet of hose. We usually work as partners, or with a pack horse. My boss drives through in his old Army jeep and drops off the heavy cans of goop so we don't have to pack them. The Forest Service wants you to spray each infested tree at least thirty feet from the ground or as high as you can see bug hits." Rex droned on about opening a five-gallon goop can, inserting the tube into the can and starting the pump, and flipping goop high up the tree with his wrist.

Brenda rolled her eyes.

"Then, you're ready to move on to the next bug tree. After you spray a lot of trees, you get paid, which is the best part of bugging! The End."

"The end of the absolute worst essay ever written about the stinky, smelly, dirty job of bugging!" I yelled.

"Debbie, that's enough!" Dad had slipped in, and he had fire in his eyes. "Bugging is how we make a living, and Rex has written a darn good paper about it. The work may be dirty, but it pays the bills!" I steeled myself for more, but he was hungry. He turned to Rex.

"You did real good, son. You ought to add that the bug hits are sometimes as high as 100 feet, and it takes a bit of muscle to get goop that high! Now, Mama, if the gravy's done, let's eat those venison steaks and mashed taters."

***

Sunday, March 12, 1967

TETON

Every Sunday, Mama took us to the sacrament meeting of the Teton Ward of The Church of Jesus Christ of Latter-day Saints.

It was boring, but we spiced it up. Shanan was on my lap, and Rex wouldn't give her any Cheerios. She giggled and pounded his arm. At home, I had curled the hair on top of her head around a tiny roller, forming one blond curl. She wore the pale blue dress that Dad had bought when I was little—he loved seeing his tiny daughters in blue—and she looked like a blond angel.

I shoved Rex.

"Hush! They're blessing a baby!" Mama whispered.

"What's *blessing*?" Shanan asked, loudly.

"It's a prayer. The baby's Daddy is giving the baby its name and a special blessing," Mama whispered.

At the front of the chapel, men stood in a circle holding a tiny infant. The proud father pronounced a blessing, then held up his son, fussing, for all to see.

"Ohhhh!" the congregation exhaled.

Andrea whispered, "Who's gonna bless our baby?"

"Mama's got plenty of brothers who can do it—Uncle Ern, Uncle Verl, Uncle Bud, or Uncle John, even Uncle Denton from Utah. Maybe the bishop," Brenda whispered back. "Remember when Shanan was blessed by Uncle Verl?"

Dad worked, hunted, or fished most Sundays. He attended church on big occasions, like Shanan's blessing in 1964, looking handsome in his suit—so different from his Levi's and blue work shirt. But that day, his cheerful self-confidence had drained to zero. He didn't walk to the front of the room with the other men. He couldn't help to bless Shanan because he wasn't a member of our church and didn't hold the Melchizedek Priesthood. My heart still broke for him, two years later.

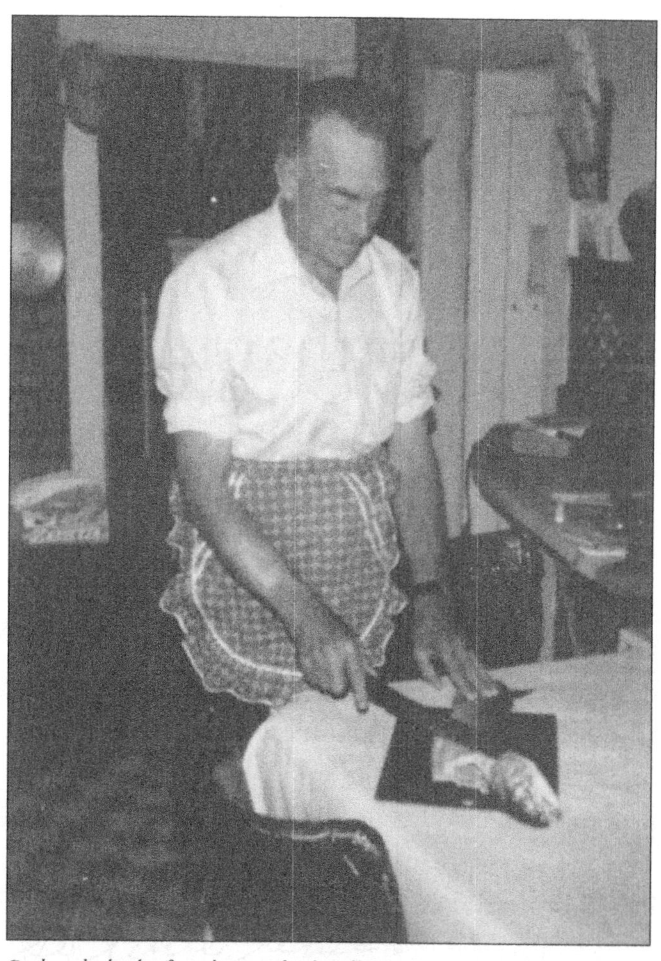

Dad made this knife with a wooden handle and a long sharp blade. An apron kept his clothes clean. He loved it when grandkids called him "Suzy" and teased him about the ruffles. Photo from the 1970s.

Abraham, Isaac, and Dad

I looked around the chapel. The presidents of the Church looked back at me out of heavy gilt frames. Only Joseph Smith and David O. McKay had no beards. Behind the pulpit was a large painting of Jesus Christ with children. It reminded me of a family picture on Wendy's living room wall, painted by Wendy's grandma—not bad, but the people had flat noses. Maybe that lady had painted this picture because the kids didn't look quite right. Anyway, Jesus looked kind. It gave me a good feeling.

A man in a suit, the stake president, said, "Arden Stewart has been called as bishop of the Teton Ward of The Church of Jesus Christ of Latter-day Saints, and we'd like to invite him to share his testimony."

Mama smiled at me. I babysat for Brother and Sister Stewart, and I liked them. They paid well—thirty-five cents an hour—and their kids were good. Mama settled Shanan in her lap and pulled Andrea close as we listened to Bishop Stewart's testimony. Mama glowed. Anything to do with church, or Jesus, made her look that way. It wasn't easy getting us kids to church twice every Sunday for Sunday school and sacrament meeting. We were always late, and we didn't make it every week, but Mama kept coming and kept smiling.

In the twelve-to-thirteen-year-old Sunday School class, Bea and Sandy were on one side of the room, comparing nail polish. Bea's matched her hot pink pull-over and short gray pleated skirt. Sandy wore a pink sweater and pleated skirt: they liked to match. I sat in a corner across the room. *Do they miss Wendy?* I wondered. She attended the Wilford Ward. My nails were bare and short—nail polish was a rarity at our house, since the older girls were gone, and Brenda chewed her nails to the quick. I wore my birthday jumper with Brenda's white blouse, which was a little big. I tugged my nylons and moved my right leg to cover up a large run on my left leg.

Seven boys between us punched each other. Nobody was listening. The teacher held up a picture of a bearded prophet holding a knife above a young man, found his place in the Bible, and read, "Take now thy son, thine only son Isaac, whom thou lovest . . . and offer him there for a burnt offering."

Whoa. I didn't know a lot about the Bible, but it seemed like God told this guy to stab and burn his son.

"Why would God do that?" I blurted.

The teacher looked up. "It was a test to see if Abraham would obey Heavenly Father by sacrificing his son."

"What good would that do? His son would be dead," I protested.

"Abraham waited many years to have a child; then God asked him to give up the most precious thing he had: Isaac. It's like Heavenly Father giving His Son, Jesus Christ, for you and for me."

I understood about Jesus—I'd heard that all my life. But I didn't see how *Isaac* being dead would do anybody any good.

The teacher added, "Of course, God stopped Abraham from killing Isaac. He put a ram in the bushes to be the sacrifice."

"I don't care. Abraham was mean!" I protested.

"He did it to obey God." Bea fluffed her curled-under hair. "I'd sacrifice a person if God asked me to."

"Really? Who?" asked the teacher.

"Debra Nelson!" The class laughed.

My face burned. I could see myself walking across the room and slapping Bea's face. Hard. That would feel good! Instead, I whispered, "Excuse me."

"Don't hurry back, or I'll come after you with a knife!" Bea announced.

I retreated to the girls' bathroom in the furthest corner

of the church and contemplated the floor—hundreds of tiny one-inch square tiles, smoother, slicker, and newer than any bathroom floor I'd ever seen.

Mama brings us to church to make us into good people, yet Bea talks about killing me, people laugh at me, and I want to hurt her. I would've been better off going ice fishing with Dad.

I believe in Jesus Christ and love Him. But this story is strange. It wasn't fair for Heavenly Father to make Abraham wait all that time for Isaac, then ask him to kill him. Even if God knew there was a ram in the bush.

So much is not fair. It isn't fair for Bea to steal Wendy away from me and be a snot to people—not only to me: she's mean to boys, too, at school and at church. It isn't fair that I don't feel that my family is as good as other people in Teton. But I should *feel that we are—Mama fights for us. She reminds us to "throw your shoulders back and walk tall, like a Nelson!" She makes sure we have clothes that are somewhat in style, clean, mended, and ironed. She pushes us to do well in school, to give talks in church, to perform in plays, and to give readings in talent shows.*

But Mama couldn't do it all. Last week's Sunday School lesson was on temple covenants. The teacher showed a picture of a radiant young couple in front of the Salt Lake Temple and said, "Active church members can make temple covenants that *seal* them together—in other words, that make their family ties eternal. Were any of your parents married in the temple, the House of the Lord?"

My hand didn't go up; most of the others' did. My stomach lurched. If any of our family died, we wouldn't be together because Mama's and Dad's marriage was "until death do you part." They hadn't married in a temple. However, families like ours could be sealed later, and that would make it like our parents had been married in the temple. Mama painted a beautiful word picture: All of us, dressed in white, kneeling around a lace-covered altar to be sealed.

I wanted that more than anything, but it was out of reach. Every person in the family had to be worthy to enter the temple, so, first, Dad needed to be baptized a member of the Church. Mama said he'd come close a few times. She loved him too much to force him.

Dad was older than most fathers of kids my age. Threads of gray showed in his brown crewcut, but he ignored them, always busy, usually cheerful. That morning, when I groused about him going ice fishing while we went to church, Mama had said, "Count your blessings. God gave you a wonderful Dad."

She was right. Dad could do anything from killing and butchering animals to managing a bugging crew, from soothing a baby to welding car parts. He rated high at telling funny stories and laughing at his kids' jokes. We loved to hear him sing, especially "The Big Rock Candy Mountain." He taught me how to bait hooks with worms, trout flies, and grasshoppers, and when I was small, he'd cast for me, "set" a fish on the line and hand the pole to me—I was smug about how many fish I caught until he decided I was old enough to fish on my own. He kept his pocketknife sharp and in his Levi's pocket, ready for any job from shaving callouses off his feet to trimming meat from the haunch of a deer. Every fall, he harvested enough wood to keep us and several Teton widows warm through the winter.

He wasn't afraid of a living man or woman. When Brenda told Mama—and Mama told Dad—that a man had abused her, Dad went straight to his home, grabbed him by the collars and threatened his life. He was downright terrifying to anyone who hurt one of his kids.

But as I stared at the tiles, I thought she was also wrong. I felt disloyal as I tallied up failings that stood out like a Yellowstone Park bear in purple pajamas because, in Teton, we were surrounded by Church members who didn't do what he did. He drank coffee every morning and a few beers over the course of the summer; he used brandy instead of cough syrup; he smoked Camels, and he swore freely. I didn't know the fathers of the kids in my Sunday School class, but, surely, they must be free of such sins.

The two sides of Dad were hard to reconcile. *Will we ever be sealed as a family?* I wondered, picking at a scab on my knee until it bled. *What if our family never makes it to the temple? It's not just Dad—I'm far from perfect. Mama spends a lot of time busting up arguments between us kids. If Rex would stop picking on me, I could do better. We might sing "Love at Home" at church, but we don't fit the perfect family pattern expected of good Latter-day Saints.*

Washing my hands with the church's good-smelling liquid soap, I pondered. *Ellen and Kerry, and Jeanne and Alan, were married in the Idaho Falls Temple. I can't change Dad, but* ***I*** *could get married there.* From the mirror, solemn green eyes told me that a temple marriage was my deepest desire. It would take years, but that might help get the rest of us sealed there, too.

The bell in the hall buzzed loudly, signaling the end of Sunday School.

At home, I changed my clothes and turned on our small black and white television.

"Turn that confounded thing off! I'm gonna put my foot through the picture tube one of these days!" Dad sat at the table, his whetstone in his left hand and a long butcher knife—fitted to a homemade wooden handle—in his right. "Go help your Mama."

I hustled past his knife into the kitchen, pronto—not because Dad ever used the thing on anything but fish, meat, and onions—but because his bark was loud.

Mama handed me a potato peeler. "What did you learn in Sunday School?"

Instead of my stock answer, "Prayer," I asked, "Mama, if God commanded Dad to sacrifice one of his kids, would he do it?"

"Oh! Did you learn about Abraham and Isaac?"

"Yeah. It was a mean thing for God to ask Abraham

to do."

Whisk, whisk, whisk went the knife on Dad's stone. Mama rinsed a spud and cut it up. "Remember: two people were involved. Maybe you should ask, 'If God commanded my father to kill me, would I go along with it, or would I fight my Dad *and* God?'"

I stared at her. I imagined myself on an altar with Dad, wielding that butcher knife above me. *I wouldn't lie quiet and let it happen, because—Dad is like Abraham in one thing—when he makes up his mind, he means business.*

Mama cut another potato. "By not resisting, Isaac did what Jesus did when He laid down on the cross and stretched out his hands, ready for the nails. Jesus had the power to get away, but He didn't. Jesus gave His life for us. And God, His Father, allowed it to happen—He sacrificed His Beloved Son." Mama's tears dripped into the sink. "I couldn't get through a day without their sacrifices. Jesus died for my sins, and Heavenly Father stood back and allowed His Son to suffer for me."

What she says is true. Heavenly Father was willing sacrifice His Son, the same as Abraham. But Dad? I thought, picking up a spud and pulling a sprout off. Spuds got soft and sprouty after winter in the basement. I tossed the sprout into the peelings.

"Maybe Heavenly Father wouldn't ask Dad to give that much—to sacrifice one of us."

"I hope God never asks Daddy and me to do that. Each of you kids is a treasure beyond belief. But God asks your dad to sacrifice his sweat, and muscle, and brains, every day. And he does. Your Dad works hard for us. Harder than you can imagine." Mama slid cut-up potatoes into boiling water, put her hands on both sides of my face, and looked into my eyes. "Why don't you worry about how *you'd* do if you were asked to give up something dear to you? Just worry about *you.*"

Dad stuck his head into the kitchen. "Look, Joyce!" He flicked the corner off a piece of paper with a flourish of the gleaming knife blade.

"That's the sharpest knife in Teton!" Mama flashed him a smile.

We have the sharpest knives in Teton, I thought, cutting the last potato with another knife honed by Dad's stone. *Not the prettiest, but the sharpest.*

Dad whistled as he carved the ham.

Mama tried to get each daughter a new dress for Easter and other special occasions. In 1960, the older girls sewed "sister dresses" for a cousin's wedding, complete with lilac-colored "gores" between the print panels, providing fulness that worked beautifully with bouffant petticoats. Pictured in front of the farmhouse in Clementsville, Idaho, from left to right: Judy, Ellen, Jeanne (they wore nylon stockings, prone to getting runners and snags), Brenda, me, and ten-month-old Andrea (we wore white anklet socks).

De Gaulle and Easter Eggs

Tuesday, March 14, 1967

TETON

Two enormous sneezes rattled my head as I buried my face in my shoulder and fumbled in my pocket for a piece of toilet paper. I shouldn't have come to school.

"Yuck! Sneezing without a tissue is the worst bad manners. Stop blowing boogers all over!" Bea said.

Wendy laughed.

"Debra DeBooger Factory," Bea yelled, and the class laughed.

I hate being called Debra almost as much I hate DeBooger Factory.

This had happened thanks to our first-grade teacher. When we arrived on the first day, there were two girls called *Debbie* who both had the given name *Debra*.

"You will be *Debbie*," she pronounced, patting the other girl's shoulder. "And you will be *Debra*," she said to me.

I didn't want to be called *Debra*; it sounded like *brat*, or *De-brat*, which Brenda and Rex called me sometimes. Yet, *Debra* it was. This year, a few of the boys called me *De-BRA*. Embarrassing!

However, Bill Briggs, our neighbor boy, called me *Debbie*. Bill was two years older than us, but he had missed a lot of school for surgeries, so he was in our sixth grade. His legs were in braces, he used crutches, and he couldn't go outside for recess. On days when he came to school, he and I got along, so I *did* have a friend. I had forgotten to count him because he was a boy and because he missed a lot of school. Bill was a cheerful soul who liked everyone, and everyone liked Bill. Even Bea, though she sometimes teased him until he looked sad. I wasn't her only target.

Bea whispered, "DeBooger Factory" to Bill, and he snorted. Everybody laughed. The slightest comical remark set Bill off, and his giggles were contagious. He couldn't help that.

"DeBooger Factory"—it *was* a little funny. I smiled and blew my nose with toilet paper.

After school, I took a long, soaky bath and a nap, and I

woke feeling better. I joined Mama and Brenda painting the high, smoke-stained walls of the living and dining rooms. While we painted, Brenda chattered about her plans to sew a dress for Friday's dance, sang a song she learned in French class, said she wanted Dad to take us deer hunting on Loon Creek (where Dad and Mama had honeymooned, far away), and informed us that they had re-buried President Kennedy's body in Arlington National Cemetery that day.

"Brenda, you missed a spot. Goodness, you're a Renaissance teenager!" Mama interrupted.

"What's that?" Andrea asked.

"A Renaissance man or woman is someone who knows a lot about many things." Mama handed Brenda a list, saying, "Take your Renaissance ideas—and Debbie, and get more paint at the Merc."

Brenda drove me the five blocks to the Teton Mercantile but stayed in the car to listen to her favorite disc jockey. At the Merc—a fancy two-story building that had once been a bank—you could buy everything from two-by-fours, to canned tomatoes, to towels. Dad's friend "Mutt" Johnson, the Merc's co-owner, sometimes asked Dad to help him cut and wrap meat for customers who brought dressed-out farm animals or wildlife to the Merc's butcher block.

I grabbed the items and hurried toward the front, with the handle of a gallon paint bucket digging into my right palm while I juggled a whole chicken and two cans of soup in my left. I was intent on dumping my load on the counter, but Bea sneaked up from the side and gently set down Wonder Bread, pink Dippity Do hair gel, and a five-dollar bill.

She cut me off! I groaned.

The clerk thanked Bea profusely, counted back her change, then rang up my items.

"Cash or charge?"

"Charge." *Why does she have to talk so loud?*

She wrote the total in her book and barked, "Your Dad's account is past due."

"He'll pay before the end of the month." Dad always paid the Merc when he got paid.

"He'd better."

My face was red, but I looked her in the eye. "He will."

Where's Mutt? I wondered. When Mutt rang up our purchases, or teased us when we bought penny candy, he never said a word about our account.

Bea stood aside as I struggled to the door with my load. As I grabbed for the handle, my paper bag ripped, dumping groceries everywhere. Bea made sure the clerk was watching, then bent graciously to help me.

Looking up from the dead chicken skittering across the doormat, my nose tickled, and I sneezed—right into Bea's face.

Diary, Sunday, March 19, 1967, Teton: Went to church and Sacrament meeting. Mama thinks she might have No. 10 tonight. God be with her.

A couple of times during March, Mama and Dad hurried to the hospital, thinking the baby was coming, but it was "false labor."

One day, Dad rolled out a map of the Targhee National Forest on the table and put salt and pepper shakers on the corners.

Mama put her hand on her back and sat down with a little grunt.

"I wonder if I'm carrying a boy," she muttered. "This pregnancy has sure been different." She was stitching a baby blue nightgown with a navy-blue necktie.

"I've got to hand it to the Forest Service. They want to keep the lodgepoles healthy, so they have us spray—it doesn't change anything for the trees the bugs have killed, but killing beetles saves the rest of the forest for recreation and logging. We've got a month to figure this out. They're awarding contracts on April 10." Dad's finger brushed the map. "We ought to bid on the West Porcupine Creek and Lower Cave Falls units. We could park the bus in this meadow. It's near both units."

Dad took good care of his bugging crew. Using his welding and carpentry skills, he'd converted an old school bus into a camper, complete with two double-sized bunk beds, a single bed, a cupboard for dishes and canned goods, a gas-powered kitchen range and fridge, a table with two bus seats for dining, and a small heating stove with a chimney. The bus was the center of *Bug Camp*, which included sleeping tents, an outdoor shower fed with buckets of water, and a latrine.

Mama read, "'Significant numbers of affected trees,' it says, on both units."

"Yup! Lot of trees means lots of money!" Dad winked at Mama. He loved bugging better than dry farming. "It'll be a great summer. We should make good money."

Six huge spruce trees in our front yard moaned in the March gale. Summer sounded good.

Rex raced in, slamming the front door and rattling the windows. "We got a letter from Bruce!"

Getting a letter from our soldier was a big deal. When the U.S. Army drafted Bruce and sent him to France in 1965, he was mad because his high school friends were fighting in Vietnam, and he wasn't. Dad told him our troops in Europe were well positioned to pick off Comrade Brezhnev, if need be, but Bruce never saw that kind of action. He sat at a desk, administering progress tests to soldiers and honing his two-fingered typing skills. Letter-writing was too much like Army work to be much fun.

Dad scanned the thin airmail paper. "Bruce will be home by April! Old de Gaulle is kicking NATO out to open the way for the Commies—that man has no gratitude for our boys who died in France in World War II. But, by golly, I'm glad Bruce will be discharged in time for bugging!"

Mama rushed from the kitchen, her hands pasty with bread dough. "Discharged? His tour's not up until May!"

"Yup, discharged! No chance he'll end up in Vietnam!" The way they hugged and kissed was embarrassing.

Diary, Monday, March 20, 1967, Teton: No new developments. Bruce wrote and said he would be home before the 6th of April. Mama made baby a darling nightie and necktie.

***

Friday, March 24, 1967

TETON

Rex and I ran to greet Jeanne and Alan after their thirteen-hour drive from the University of Idaho. "It feels like forever since Christmas!" Jeanne hugged five people at once. We swept them into the house, Alan and Rex laden with bags.

Jeanne helped us make Easter baskets from cottage cheese cartons and crepe paper. Then she and Mama rolled out pies for the next day. We dropped into bed, exhausted.

At 1:30 a.m., I woke up to go to the bathroom. Mama puttered in the kitchen, chopping vegetables for turkey dressing and "putting in a nightshift," as she called it. Our Easter baskets sat empty.

"Hey, you haven't done anything with our Easter

baskets yet! Want me to fill them?"

"Sure. Don't eat all of the malted milk eggs!" She handed me the bag, and I popped several into my mouth while dumping the rest into baskets.

A slight sound made me jump as I opened the jelly-beans. *Did somebody open the back door? Probably the dog.*

Then Bruce was there, whispering, "Mom!"

Mama turned with a start, color draining from her face. Her hands went to her round tummy. Mama was usually fun to surprise—squealing and punching Bruce's arm—but something was different this time. She seemed nervous and preoccupied. I'd never seen her like this. Two nights before, she'd been to the hospital with false labor. That thing pinged in my stomach.

Bruce, Rex, and Patches in the orchard next to our home in Teton; about 1965.

River Secrets

Bruce felt it, too. "Aww, Mom, I'm sorry. How are you? I shouldn't have scared you. I wanted to surprise you, so I had Theron pick me up at the bus terminal in Salt Lake City and bring me here."

Mama nuzzled into his arms and held him tight. "It's all right; you're home! God bless Theron, that wonderful cousin of yours. Daddy and I didn't know how we'd get you home!"

Dad rushed in, wearing his sleeveless undershirt and pulling on jeans, and soon everyone was awake, hugging, talking, and milling around our soldier. Bruce smelled like Brylcreem and sweat after his journey—happy, tired, and cussing Charles de Gaulle. I felt shy around him. We finally got back to bed, Bruce and Rex bunking together in the boys' room.

A dim Easter sun dawned on sloppy snow. We gobbled

candy eggs and listened to Bruce's stories about France. At dinner, the house bulged with family. After Bruce and his girlfriend slipped away, Mama quietly asked Alan and Kerry to step into her bedroom to give her a priesthood blessing. She invited Dad, but he needed to change the oil in the Ford Fairlane.

I'd never seen a priesthood blessing, and I wondered what our always-teasing brothers-in-law would do. They poured a drop of consecrated oil on the crown of Mama's head, rested their hands there, and a hush settled. Our eyes closed and their voices, first Kerry's solemn bass, then Alan's higher pitched tone, blessed Mama. Alan promised that our baby would have a safe delivery, and that through her faith in Jesus Christ, Mama would have the peace and strength she needed for the future. When they finished, Mama's eyes were wet and radiant. We floated in a sea of calm.

The family filed out, and Mama and I sat together, reveling in the beauty of the blessing. Mama sank her head into her pillow, saying, "Don't let me rest long. I need to close my eyes for five minutes."

That gut feeling came back. What if Mama died in childbirth? I'd heard stories of pioneers and even modern women who had died. Or got very sick. Yet the blessing had promised—*promised*—that she would have a safe delivery. What was I worried about?

Diary, Wednesday, April 5, 1967: Terrible head cold. Cloudy skies. Went to Primary. Brenda and I rode horse.

Mopped dining room floor. It doesn't sound like much, but boy am I tired.

Through the clouds, Brenda caught a whiff of spring. After a few false starts, we trapped our horse, Cloudy, in a corner of the apple orchard-pasture, enticing her with a bucket of oats. I'd never saddled a horse, and Brenda was rusty, but she never gave up.

"She'll cooperate to get oats," Brenda said. "She's fattening up to carry goop cans this summer. Hey, guess what? Dad said maybe I can be the cook at bug camp."

We rode double, straddled across Cloudy's broad back.

"What would you think of a boyfriend who looks like George Harrison, only with Paul McCartney's smile and no Beetles haircut?" I asked. My words jogged out as Cloudy's feet thump-thumped down the road.

"Why no haircut? That's what makes the Beetles *the Beetles*." Brenda was an expert. In 1964, she had asked me to seal her in a box and send it to the Fab Four.

"Because they're into drugs. Everybody says those long-haired guys take drugs."

"You mean Dad says that. They're handsome and rich, drugs or no drugs. We're not going to date guys who take drugs, though. That's worse than drinking."

Brenda climbed down, and Cloudy sniffed the frozen grass. I slid off, stumbling as my leg muscles cramped a bit. We watched the slate-gray Teton River boil past, bloated with snowmelt. The powerful current was frightening under its hypnotic surface.

"Will things change much when the baby comes?" I asked. Brenda was a reliable source, sharing the knowledge she soaked up from reading, school, and even movies. Last summer when my period started, Brenda taught me what to do—with Mama's blessing.

"Nahh. It'll be fun, having a little one. Shanan's getting big. It means more work—more diapers to wash. If it's a boy, he'll pee all over us!" She grinned.

"Having a new baby will be alright. I wish..." I picked up a willow stick and stripped off its leaves. "I wish school would change. I wish some fathead girls would move out of town." Tears trembled near the surface. We'd played softball in physical education that day, and Bea razzed me every time I touched the ball.

"Listen, Debbie. Mama's going to have a new baby—maybe a boy! We'll be happy. We always are with a baby in the house. When school's out, we'll move to the farm, and the Teton kids can go suck eggs."

Tears popped into my eyes. That bad feeling nagged my gut, and it had nothing to do with Bea.

"Brenda, will Mama be okay?" I whispered.

She didn't look startled. "I dunno." She nibbled a fingernail. "She's had nine kids and been fine—I'm pretty sure everything will work out. Her priesthood blessing promised she'd have a safe delivery."

My stick whistled as I flung it into the water.

Brenda launched her stick, hard.

The river drowned our willows, sweeping them under the bridge.

Diary, Thursday, April 6, 1967: What a day! First, I hit a single in P.E. Mom had a baby girl 6 lb. 11 oz. NOW I'm so happy. WOW GEE WOW—GOSH!!

Later, Dad told us that our newborn sister had an enlarged heart and an undeveloped ear. For most of our lives, that was all we knew about her condition.

Diary, Friday, April 7, 1967: I stayed home and tended Shanan. The baby has an enlarged heart and her ear isn't completely formed. Dad took her to Idaho Falls, now to Salt Lake.

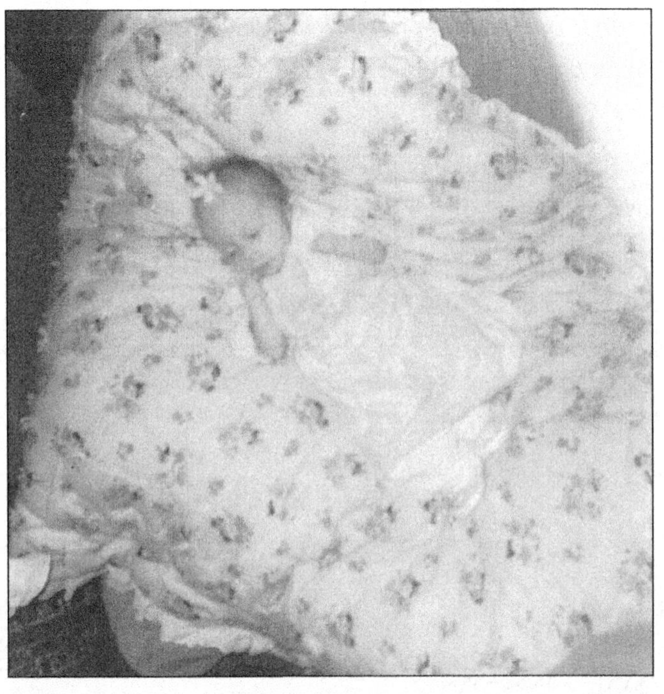

Holly Joyce Nelson was born on April 6, 1967. She weighed six pounds and eleven ounces. In this photo, she was about six weeks old.

Holly Joyce Nelson

The next portion of Holly's story follows her as Dad took her far from Mama and the rest of us. Conversations with Mama, Dr. Ronald Lechelt, family members, photos, and letters preserved over the years form the basis of this chapter.

Holly was born at 5:10 p.m. on April 6, 1967, in Ashton Memorial Hospital. Mama had given birth to nine healthy children, all of whom cried loudly and nursed hungrily. Holly did neither, although she was full-term and weighed six pounds, eleven ounces. Holly struggled to breathe.

Mama had lived under a cloud of worry throughout this pregnancy, and in the brief moments before the nurse took the baby away, she saw that Holly's left ear hadn't developed. It was folded into the side of her head like a partially opened rosebud. As the nurse whisked Holly out of the delivery room, Mama thought, "Our other babies had the prettiest, sweetest little ears—oh, this poor little one!"

Dr. Willis Melcher, our family doctor, brought Dad into Mama's room half an hour later. "Your baby is having trouble breathing, so we're giving her oxygen. Otherwise, her condition is stable." He paused. "She... she presents several symptoms beyond my ability to treat. I want to send her to the LDS Hospital in Idaho Falls."

Mama's face blanched. Dad's arm tightened around her shoulders.

The doctor continued, "Wayne, you told me once how you safely welded a puncture in a car's gas tank. You know how to handle oxygen. All we could do for the baby in an ambulance would be to administer oxygen, so if we can get an oxygen tank into your car, you could transport her yourself if you have someone to drive."

"I'll call my son. We've got an oxygen tank at home."

"Use the phone at the nurse's station. Joyce, I hope you can rest now."

Dad phoned Bruce, and then Judy, who agreed to meet them at the hospital in Idaho Falls. Someone called Ellen, tending children for the Zollinger family in Rexburg. Then Dad went to the hospital gift shop and purchased a bouquet: eight red roses and two white roses.

Mama managed a grateful smile.

"Red roses for our eight daughters and white roses for

our two sons," Dad whispered. He seldom gave Mama florist's flowers, but he picked wildflowers for her in the summer and brought her the first daffodils of spring from the supermarket.

"Wayne, see if you can get someone to bless the baby in Idaho Falls. Let's name her Holly—it means *holy.*"

Two nurses carried Holly in a glass isolette to the backseat of our Ford Fairlane, where Dad leaned over to hold a tiny oxygen tube near her nose. With Bruce driving, they arrived in Idaho Falls an hour later.

Dr. Ronald Lechelt, the pediatrician on call in the LDS Hospital Emergency Room, gently touched Holly's body, feeling the strain of her efforts to breathe, listening, and observing. He was in his thirties and had practiced pediatrics in Idaho Falls for eight years. He grew up in Iowa but came west when a medical school friend, Reid Fife, told him of Idaho's great skiing. Ronald and Reid would practice together for decades.

Dad, Bruce, Silver, and Judy huddled together in the waiting room. When Dr. Lechelt entered, there was palpable silence as they turned to him.

"Your baby—Holly, you said? The x-rays show that Holly's heart is enlarged, crowding her lungs. There are other issues. She needs special care. I'm going to send her to Salt Lake City, to Dr. George Veasy. He grew up here—he was a partner of my partner, Dr. Fife; they were classmates in high school. He specializes in pediatric cardiology, and he's one of the smartest and kindest individuals I know. You can transport her to Primary Children's Hospital the same way you brought her here."

Dad cleared his throat. He felt awkward, but he would ask, for Mama. He must, or this baby might die without a blessing, and he wasn't sure what that might mean for her eternal soul. "My wife, in Ashton, she wondered if...if we could make sure that Holly gets her name and blessing."

"The nurses are feeding Holly, and I need to call Dr. Veasy. I understand that blessings are important for infants in your church. She can be blessed if someone can do it quickly after her feeding." Dr. Lechelt shook Dad's hand and slipped away.

Judy pulled a nurse aside. "Are there LDS elders here tonight who could give my sister a blessing?"

The nurse shook her head. "I don't think so. It's late for visitors."

"May I look around? Missionaries sometimes visit patients during the evening," Judy asked.

"Sure, check at all the nurses' stations." The nurse turned away.

Dad watched his oldest daughter walk away. Would Judy find anyone who could bless Holly? Was Judy's heart hurting like his? Did Bruce and Silver feel this consuming pain that cried out for heavenly help? Dad slumped in his chair and ran his hands through his crew-cut. Bruce and Silver stared into the stormy night.

Tiny Holly's need was broader than any barrier

between each of these beloved ones and God. Invisible tendrils of love twined through the air from her tiny self, touching hearts.

Judy, eight months pregnant, implored the Lord to guide her to priesthood holders who could bless Holly. Dad remembered his mother's favorite hymn and asked the *Rock of Ages* to send someone to help Holly receive her name and a blessing, to help her live, and to watch over Mama. Bruce closed his eyes and pleaded for Holly, reaching back to childhood prayers for words. Silver mentally repeated the rosary, remembering the tenderness on his mother's face as she fingered her beads.

Judy glimpsed someone in a dark suit go around a corner and quickened her pace. In a few minutes, she led two missionaries to the waiting room. A nurse ushered the group to the examining room, where another nurse had coaxed drops of formula into Holly's mouth with an eyedropper.

"She tried, and now she's too tired swallow," the attending nurse said. "Dr. Lechelt is still busy. This is a good time for her to be blessed."

Elder Frank Brown asked, "What would you like to name your baby?"

Dad rubbed a callous on his left hand. "Well, Holly, of course, because she's holy, like her Mama says. And she's her Mama's eighth daughter, and she's beautiful—like Joyce. Holly Joyce Nelson."

Surrounded by loving family and heaven-sent strangers, Holly received her name and a priesthood blessing.

As the nurses prepared to move Holly's glass isolette to the back seat of the Ford, Judy said, "I'll go with you to Salt Lake, Dad. I'm a nurse, and I can talk with the doctors."

"No, Judy. You've got Michael to think of—and that little one you're carrying." Dad was firm.

Silver agreed, tightening his arm around Judy's shoulder. "Judy, Holly will be surrounded by nurses and doctors. When your Mom comes home, she'll need *you*. Take Michael tomorrow, and go see your Mom."

***

The Fairlane sped south on Idaho Highway 191, almost the only vehicle under the stormy sky. Dad's fingers trembled as he held the oxygen tube near Holly's nose—he hadn't had a smoke for hours. He could live without a cigarette—his newborn child was fighting to master the delicate art of breathing. He wished he'd thrown them away long ago.

He thought of Mama in the hospital 271 miles away. She'd be weeping, her anxiety for Holly replaying in constant loops; she excelled at worrying about her children. He had heard a nurse tell her that they would bind her breasts to reduce the flow of colostrum and breastmilk. Beneath the bands, he knew, her yearning heart would not be bound.

Dad and Bruce loved to visit with each other, but miles slipped by in silence. Untold stories of Bruce's stint in France and anecdotes from last year's bugging, hunting, and fishing would wait.

Finally, Bruce asked, "Hey, Dad, do you know the way to the hospital?"

"Why—I've heard of it, of course, the kids collect pennies for it every year, but all I know is that it's on a hill near the Utah Capitol building. North side of town. Hey, do you want me to drive? Traffic's getting thick."

"Nah. I've been in France where they drive crazy! At least these cars are driving on the right side of the road!"

Close to Salt Lake City, they saw a sign: "Primary Children's Hospital Next Exit." They took the exit, and there was another sign—time after time, when they wondered where to go, a sign appeared. Traffic lights turned green as they approached.

***

Friday, April 7, 1967

SALT LAKE CITY, UTAH

Nurses moved Holly into an examination room at 2:03 a.m. Dad and Bruce sat in the waiting room, feeling empty, trying to doze. The clock ticked out the long minutes.

A doctor came in.

"Hello, I'm Dr. S."

"I'm Wayne Nelson from Teton, Idaho, and this is my son, Bruce."

Dr. S. shook their hands. "I'll do a complete examination of your infant. We will talk again when I have finished." He walked back through the door marked *Medical Staff Only*.

"What do you want me to do, Dad? Should I stay with you?" Bruce asked.

"No, you'd better not. Mama's going to need you. I don't know how long I'll need to stay. I'll get a motel room, but I'll need the car." Dad rubbed his chin.

"A few days ago, I was here, and I saw that there's a bus headed north at 7:00 a.m."

Dad smiled. "You've got it all figured out. I hate to leave Holly here at the hospital while I drive you to the bus station."

Bruce stood up. "No big deal. It can't be more than three-quarters of a mile from here. But I better get hiking."

"You'll need a ticket." Dad pulled out his well-worn wallet.

Bruce waved him away. "No need. It's on Uncle Sam."

They hugged, and Bruce was gone.

Dad stood at the window watching his son cross the grounds, remembering the day Bruce left for basic training. How afraid he and Mama had been that Bruce would end up under fire in a jungle halfway around the world! This time Bruce wasn't offering to risk his life, but frail Holly was fighting a battle for her life—far from her Mama and the rest of her big family. Loneliness washed over him.

The Salt Lake Valley was waking, although the Wasatch Mountains blocked the sunrise. Dad could see the dome of the Utah State Capital Building and the spires of the Salt Lake Temple. Headlights traced the grids of hundreds of streets.

Some quail flew into a bush near the streetlight. Quail were creatures that Dad understood in this foreign place—pecking for food, reveling in short flights, guarding their little ones. At any hint of danger, they skittered to safety under thick juniper bushes, steering their chicks in front of them.

He turned from the quail and followed a hallway to a plate glass window into a nursery—not the nursery of magazine cartoons, where relieved fathers wave at chubby offspring, but an intensive care nursery full of gravely ill infants. He scanned the babies and spotted a portly, gray-haired nurse taking Holly's pulse. Holly had an oxygen tube at her nose and a feeding tube down her throat. Less than twenty-four hours ago, she had been curled, safe in Mama's womb, safe, safe, Mama's heart beating for Holly's enlarged heart, Mama keeping her alive and cradling her from harm.

Dr. S. walked through the door. "Mr. Nelson, I've

examined your infant. It has an enlarged heart and—the unformed ear. My colleague, Dr. Veasy, who I believe to be the top pediatric cardiologist west of the Mississippi, will do a full examination later today."

"I'm glad she's getting the best doctor there is. That's a comfort."

"Similar to her left ear, the baby's kidneys are undeveloped. The two conditions go together. Other organs most likely have abnormalities."

"Wh—what caused it?"

"It could stem from several different causes—we don't know the exact origin of her problems."

Dad scratched his chin—whiskers growing, he'd had no time to shave. Had he packed his razor?

The doctor coughed and asked, "You are—how old?"

Dad jerked back to reality. His spine stiffened. "I'm fifty."

"And your wife?"

"She's forty-six."

The doctor's eyebrows lifted as he charted their ages.

"When parents are over forty, congenital issues are exacerbated. As I said, Dr. Veasy will examine it. There's no hope that it will live more than a few days."

Dad offered his calloused hand, which Dr. S. shook. Then he slid Holly's notes to the bottom of his stack and walked away.

Dad's hand tightened into a fist and punched his other hand hard. Holly would die soon. He thought it, too—he'd seen enough ill people to know when a person was losing the fight for life. He'd been with his father when he died a few years before. Yet this doctor said those words, not about *Holly*—the brunette girl given a beautiful name and a blessing by Elder Frank Brown—but about *it*.

Dad looked through the glass at Holly. The left side of her face was turned toward him, and her hairline traced the same contour as his hairline. He looked at her left ear enfolded into the skin of her head and remembered the nine times he and Mama had reveled in new babies, examining each one in its unique perfection. Holly wasn't perfect, yet somehow, she was wondrous. Across the miles, he felt Mama's love for Holly—because she was theirs, yes, but also because she was different—because she struggled. Mama's fists clenched with fierce love for all who struggled, like Holly's tiny fists clenched.

Everything in him yearned toward this child of his middle age. It wasn't as if he and Mama didn't know where their babies came from. Something inside them said, "Be fruitful, multiply, replenish," and they did and loved the harvest. Their love for each other pulsated to the rhythm of the world around them, and they produced children who flourished, lived—and were treasured. Like quail mothers gathering their chicks, they embraced every baby that came—Dad by working with all his might to make a living, and Mama by supervising the flight patterns of a brood that ranged from chick to adult.

Mama overflowed with joyful, spontaneous motherly love, honed to perfection over twenty-six years. Like quail, they had mated for life.

Down the hall, nurses chatted as they changed shifts. The nurse that had taken Holly's pulse walked by wearily, pulling on a jacket, and smiled at him.

She's dedicated, coming to work every day to care for these babies. Maybe Dr. S.'s gruffness is a shield to help him—in his own way—to deal with the heartache that haunts this nursery.

Dad walked to the window. The quail hen and her brood were out. In Idaho, a large covey of quail lived among the farm canyon's plentiful seeds and cover. He depended on quail for an occasional meal, as did circling hawks and hidden foxes. He had killed, cleaned, and eaten many quail. They had tiny, soft feathers, hard to pluck, and wee organs—infinitely intricate. Every time he cleaned a quail, he felt a prayer of thanksgiving to God for the quail's good, simple life in God's world, to be consumed by man, for man's strength.

Below, the hen clucked softly, pulling her chicks under her wings.

Dad pressed his face to the window as his tears fell.

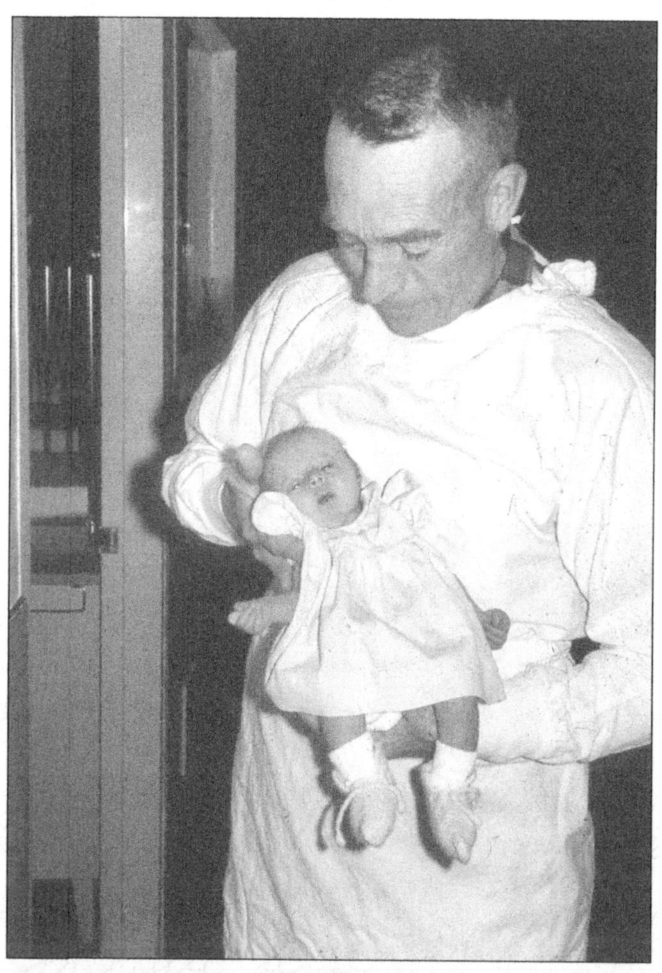

Dad and Holly at Primary Children's Hospital in Salt Lake City in April 1967. In a sweet letter, he wrote, "I got to hold her.... I know she knew she was being held and loved and it was a great privilege for me. She cried when she was put back in the isolette."

Dad's Letter

Saturday, April 8, 1967

Today I got this paper to write my family a letter. But now there isn't time to send it. I must stay until Monday and then go home. A few arrangements at the hospital still to be made. And then how can I tell them we can't have our little darling very long. The best baby doctors there is tell me the little undeveloped ear is always linked with like kidneys. Her heart is so big it compresses her left lung. The doctors hold forth no hope.

I don't know how one can learn to love a little stranger in so little time.

Bruce went home on the bus and I found out about the baby about two hours after he left. I have never been so alone in my life.

In a little while I'll go up to the hospital and see her and love her while she is here.

I just can't give up that little doll.

Sun. morning.

She doesn't look quite so good this morning. I got to hold her while the nurse changed her bed. When I picked her up, she opened her eyes and made little smacking sounds. She kept her eyes open all the time she was held, looking all she could, and it just seemed like she was saying, "I thought I had a family, where have you been?"

I know she knew she was being held and loved and it was a great privilege for me. She cried when she was put back in the isolette.

Talked to Dr. Veasy tonight and there is no longer any doubt—or hope—for our baby.

Will call Jeanne and Alan, Clara and Darrell, and Denton and let them know.

Primary Hospital sits on a mountain on the edge of Salt Lake Valley. It's high up out of the smog so these kids will have clean air. From here you can look down on the Capitol Building, the temple and all over Salt Lake. It's a beautiful sight, day or night.

Someone has startled a covey of quail and they run about on this lawn and all the lawns near here, a pleasure for all who see them. And I imagine it's the safest place in the world for them to be. [End]

I know she knew she was
being held and loved and it
was a great privilege for me.
She cried when she was put
back in the isolette.

Talked to Dr Veasy tonight and
there is no longer any doubt —
or hope for our baby

Dad's handwriting in an excerpt from a letter he wrote in Salt Lake City, April 1967.

Sat. APRIL 8

19 Baby was blessed at 12:00 – name is Holly Joyce. In serious condition at Primary Childrens Hospital. Kerry stayed with us – had wiener roast

Sun. APRIL 9

19 Holly's heart is pressing on her left lung. Mom came home today. Gen. Con. Judy & Mike came. We all had family prayer for Holly.

This scan of my diary page from April, 1967, proves that my handwriting was atrocious. It says: "Saturday April 8: Baby was blessed at 12:00. Name is Holly Joyce. In serious condition at Primary Children's Hospital. Kerry stayed with us – had wiener roast. Sunday April 9: Holly's heart is pressing on her left lung. Mom came home today. Gen[eral] Con[ference] Judy and Mike came. We all had family prayer for Holly."

When Tears Become Words

In Salt Lake City and Ashton, our parents dealt with all-consuming anguish over the health of their tiny daughter. A cloud hung over us at home, even as life continued in familiar paths.

***

Saturday, April 8, 1967

TETON

"Deb! I'm starving! Fix supper!" Brenda shouted, her hand over the phone. She giggled into the receiver, "Not you. I'm trying to make my sister do some work for a change!"

"Are you on the phone with that lazy disc jockey?" I yelled.

She shoved me into the kitchen while the DJ of the local radio station rattled out a commercial.

I didn't hear the knock at the door, but Andrea, staring at the *Gary Moore Show,* did. She shrieked with joy when Kerry rumbled, "I bet nobody around here wants to have a hotdog roast! And play softball!"

We tumbled into the cold spring evening, pulling on coats. Rex cut willow branches for roasting sticks while I gathered wood, and Kerry prepared tinder and wood for a fire at the end of the long dirt driveway. The cold air thrummed with the excitement of delicious food and a warm and crackling way to cook it.

Andrea shadowed Kerry, firing questions. "Where's Ellen?"

"Still tending those Zollinger kids." Kerry blew on glowing sparks.

"Did you know Holly is at Primary Children's Hopsital? It's the best hopsital. We collect pennies for it in the Penny Parade."

We proudly clanged pennies, nickels, and dimes into a metal bank shaped like the Primary Children's Hospital on the Wednesday nearest our birthdays at Primary, a children's after-school activity sponsored by the Church. Primary leaders shared stories about children who were comforted and healed at the haven dedicated to the principles of the Master Healer.

Andrea chattered, "I gave fourteen pennies on my birthday—two for every year, and I turned seven. The doctors at Primary Hopsital can make Holly better."

Dad never told her that Holly might die, I thought. *She doesn't know.* I opened my mouth to say, "Those doctors can't help Holly," but what came out was, "Hos-pit-al, Andi. Don't be so stupid! Honestly, what a dumb kid." Andrea's feet and tongue stopped. She looked at me. I could almost feel the lump swelling in her throat.

"Maybe I don't say it right, but I *want* the hopsital to make Holly better," she choked.

"Cut it out, Deb!" Kerry said. I felt horrible. Kerry had never reprimanded me.

"Deb, you're a smart aleck, but really you're a dumb aleck," Rex jeered. He grabbed my right hand and hit my face with it, asking, "Like it? Like it?"

"No, NO!" I yelled, trying to twist my wrist out of his grasp, "NO! I don't like it!"

"Better learn to like it!" He persisted. "Like it?"

"Okay, I like it, you big, fat meanie!" I yelled.

"Better have some more!" and with a last swipe, he let go of my wrist.

Kerry gave us a hard look. "You two settle down, or I'll pack up the hotdogs and head home."

Rex mumbled, "Sorry, sis, here's a stick." He gave me his willow stick and started to sharpen another. Andrea wiped chilly tears from her face as she took the hotdog Kerry had roasted to perfection, and I handed her a bun with a small smear of catsup—the way she liked it.

I guess Andrea doesn't need to know, I thought. *Maybe Holly won't die. Maybe she WILL be healed at Primary Children's.* It felt good to hope for it, anyway. Brenda showed Andrea how to hold Rex's mitt, and we played softball in the twilight. I fanned out and dropped the ball, but nobody seemed to care.

***

The next day—oh joy—Mama came home!

Judy settled her on the couch with Shanan at her side, and whenever she could, Mama grabbed a snuggle from wiggly Michael.

"I made soup. Why don't we eat it while we watch general conference?" Judy offered. Every April and October, our church leaders shared guidance on television, and there was nothing better than listening to them while we ate. I handed Mama a bowl of soup.

"Thanks! I need to build up my strength so I can go be with Holly."

Mama looks bad. I don't think she's strong enough to go to Salt Lake, I thought. She was pale, and her eyes sunk into deep bluish circles. Tears streamed down her face as she tried to listen to President David O. McKay's wit and comforting sermon. President McKay was in Salt Lake City. So were Holly and Dad.

That evening, Dad called. Holly had been moved

from the intensive care unit to the infant nursery. I wrote, *Holly's heart is pressing on her left lung. We all had family prayer for Holly.*

My diary, where I had recorded boring everyday events, suddenly became my lifeline: a place to write what I couldn't say out loud. A place where my tears turned into words:

Monday, April 10, 1967: Dad came home from Salt Lake. Holly Joyce doesn't have a chance to live. She is pure and sinless. Death will come as a blessing.

Tuesday, April 11, 1967: Baby is the same and losing weight. Faith and prayers are the only things we can do. She has the world's best heart doctor.

Wednesday, April 12, 1967: Baby is same. How can I say what I feel? Joy, and grief, and pain. The world is brighter, though. I helped Mama and cleaned the girls' room.

***

Wednesday, April 12, 1967

TETON

"Where'd you get those ratty shoes?" Bea jeered as we moved into the hall for recess.

I thought Jeanne's old Keds looked pretty good. No holes yet.

Bea moved her stylish pale blue flats to stomp on my feet—one of her favorite tricks. I scrambled to run out the schoolhouse door. Boy, was I glad those Keds still had good traction!

She nearly caught me, but the boys came out. She snatched a boy's woolen cap and yelled to Sandy and Wendy to come play keep-away.

I ran to the edge of the schoolyard, where patches of snow dotted the lifeless grass and walked warily, watching for Bea, and praying. *Dear Father in Heaven, please make Bea leave me alone. Help the doctors and nurses know what to do so Holly can live. Help Mama get well enough to go to see her. Help me know what to do about my pimples. Help me find a friend. Thanks, Father, for dandelion leaves coming up at the edge of the pavement. And thank you that the snow is melting! Finally.*

Somebody yelled as Bea threw the cap into a tree.

Heavenly Father, please don't help Bea. Hating Bea came so naturally that it was part of my prayer, a prayer that hovered above my head. Even the pale sun warming the air couldn't pierce the thick membrane of sadness around my heart.

Recess ended, and I ran back in time to catch a sneer from Bea as she tossed my gloves—I must've dropped one—into the trashcan. Doggone it! Two fingers had holes, but they were the only gloves I had.

Social Studies dragged on slower than a snail in peanut butter. When the last bell rang, I bolted. I could hear Andrea yelling my name, but I didn't wait. *It's only two blocks. She'll find her way.*

When I walked in our front door, Mama hugged me—it felt like the first time in a long time, though I knew that wasn't true.

"What's wrong, honey?"

"Nothing."

What could I say? "Our baby is dying," or "The kids at school hate me," or "I have zits all over my face."

I wanted to melt into her arms and sob, but the phone rang.

After she said "Hello," Mama fought tears again—must be another relative asking about Holly. She put her hand over the phone. "Where's Andrea?"

"Coming." I slammed the back door and headed for the mill race canal.

The water flowed to the falls as smooth as forest green satin, tipped over the edge, and shattered into a maelstrom of tattered lace, roaring out the voice of desolation. Thirty feet below the one-plank bridge across the canal, water spiraled into a dark whirlpool fringed with scraps of dirty foam.

The Teton Flour Mill was built by George Briggs Sr. in 1890, the same year he built the house where we lived. The mill wheel was powered by mill race canal water going over a waterfall (obscured by the tree on the left). The Briggs family milled flour, corn meal, and other grains until about 1964. The dark green treetop is a Norway spruce tree in our front yard.

A Shining Ray

Brenda and Rex had crossed the plank bridge many times. But not scaredy-cat me. Instead, I crossed the big wooden bridge where the Briggs family drove their tractors, then walked down the hill to the mill pool. Luckily, none of the Briggs boys, or anyone else, was around. Dark clouds swirled in my head like turbid water.

I'm sick of Bea picking on me. "Stand up to her," Brenda says. I'm such a chicken. I'll never stand up to her or her stinkin' sidekicks. I closed my eyes to visualize Bea's cruelties. The more I tried, the more I saw Andrea's blue eyes, filled with tears so often lately. Feeling sucker punched, I almost cried. Mama told us, "You're never alone," but today, God seemed distant.

Am I kidding? I'm as bad as Bea. I dig at Andrea 'til she cries. Rex and Brenda think they're high and mighty, so I say things to them that are worse than what Bea says to me. No wonder I don't have friends.

Mama also said, "The best time to pray is when you don't feel like praying." I sighed. *All right. I'll pray again.*

Dear Heavenly Father. I'm sorry for being such a creep to Andrea. And, yeah, Rex and Brenda. I can't talk to Mama—she's so worried about Holly. She says Holly's ear is curled inside her head. What does that look like? Will I even get to see Holly? How can we go on if she dies—if any member of our family dies? Old people die—Grandma Rhodie died three years ago, and we still miss her. Especially Mama. I prayed for Grandma to live, but she died. Will it be the same with Holly?

I sat on a rock, sobbing, watching a willow branch tumble over the falls and roil in the whirlpool, feeling equally buffeted and tossed. The stick bobbed into shallow water near my feet.

I dried my raw cheeks on my sleeve and sucked in a breath.

A red-winged blackbird trilled, telling the world spring was on the way.

My nostrils filled with a scent of green things poking up from the wet earth. The sun warmed my face. A surprisingly warm breeze ruffled my hair.

I listened to my breathing slow down. Inside, I reached upward. Something shifted.

Darkness lifted out of my head and floated away.

Light and a feeling of lightness, like the world weighed

nothing, flowed into me and through me.

This was the Holy Ghost, the Comforter that Mama talked about.

I didn't know how anything would turn out—including me—but I felt peace for the first time in a long while. I felt clean. God knew all about Holly and our family, and He understood.

***

Friday, April 14, 1967

TETON

"Ellen, you shouldn't come to Salt Lake." Mama's voice trembled. She was packing, pushing herself eight days after childbirth, still drying up her milk supply. She asked Andrea to bring her a dry washcloth to put inside her bra, for her breasts prickled and leaked every time she thought of Holly.

"I'm going! I nearly went nuts tending those kids. I couldn't help you one bit," Ellen said. "I was stuck. Finally, I can help!"

"Honey, you mustn't. What about your little one?" Mama feared that Holly would die without hearing her mother's voice or feeling her caress. She feared that she had caused Holly's impairments, and now her fear extended to Judy's and Ellen's unborn babies.

"Fiddlesticks! My baby is fine—he or she is safe inside, not due for two and a half months. I'm packed. It doesn't take long when you only have three maternity outfits!"

"Where'd you get your stubborn sassiness?" Dad asked Ellen, punching her arm lightly.

"From you!"

"Mama, we better let her come—we know better than to fight her when her mind is made up," Dad said.

When Mama and Dad were ready, Mama took Brenda's face in her hands and looked into her eyes. "Thank you for being such a good helper, honey. We trust you. You'll handle it fine. I love you." She did the same with Rex, me, and Andrea, and we hugged Dad and Ellen.

They would take Shanan to Judy's. Judy took care of Shanan and Michael in her tiny trailer home in Fort Hall, tackling potty training for both toddlers.

Ellen drove, even though she had no experience with city driving. Her cock-sure confidence eased their stress as they pondered what they would face at the end of their journey.

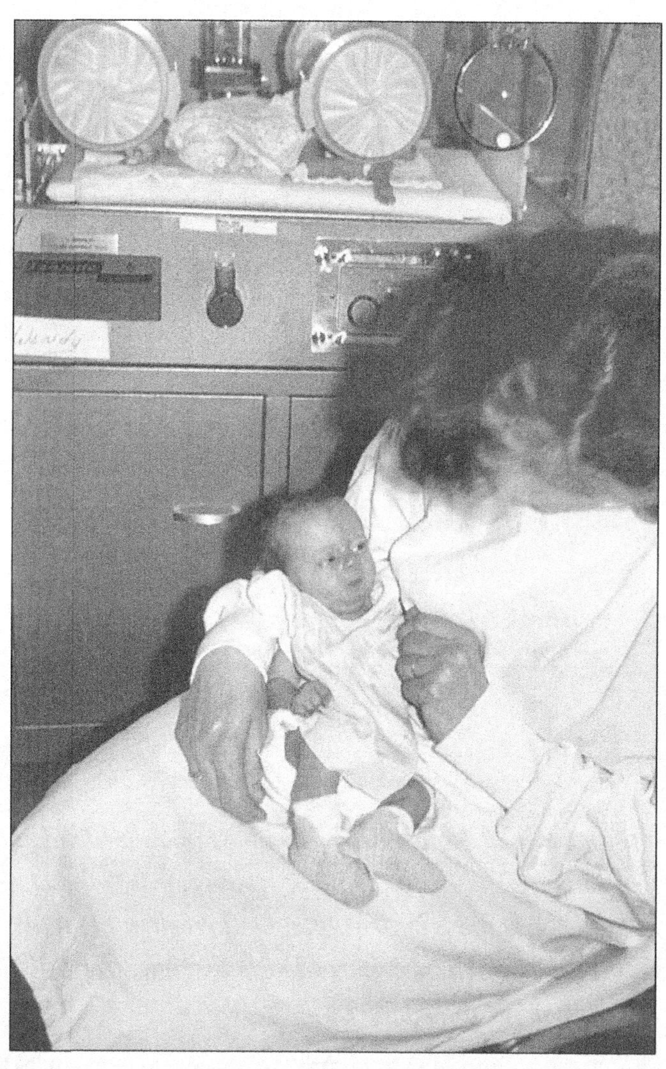

It is sweet to see Holly looking at her Mama at Primary Children's Hospital in Salt Lake City in April of 1967. Another baby is in the isolette in the background.

Knitted Together In The Womb

Friday, April 14, and Saturday, April 15; possibly other dates in April of 1967

SALT LAKE CITY

This portion of Holly's story follows Mama and Dad as they conferred with doctors about Holly's case in Salt Lake City. Conversations with Mama, Dr. Lechelt, and family members, and letters preserved over the years, form the foundation for this chapter.

Mama and Dad talked to four doctors who repeated that Holly would not live long. The doctors didn't know much about Holly's condition—there weren't adequate tests to diagnose it in 1967, and there were no surgeries or treatments that promised help. Many of Holly's organs were compromised and could not support long-term life or growth.

The nurses kindly allowed Mama to hold and feed Holly whenever they could, then she and Dad watched Holly through the window until visiting hours ended, and the nurses hinted that they should get some rest.

They went to the motel room where Ellen had returned earlier. She was sleeping soundly.

Mama had held back her tears all day, consumed by the hopelessness of Holly's case, and now they gushed out. "Seeing her—looking at her for the first time—things aren't right. That little left ear!" Dad handed Mama two tissues. "Her legs cross most of the time. When I talked to her, she, she couldn't focus her eyes at me, and her right eye doesn't want to open."

Dad sighed. "Yes. The soft spot on her head is bigger than our other kids' were. Or at least it is shaped different."

"Wayne, that doctor called Holly's condition a 'chromosome deficiency.' You know what that means! There's something wrong with us, with what we pass on to our children." Her shoulders shook, and Dad put his arm around her.

Dr. S.'s words echoed in their minds: "It has everything in the book wrong with it. You can tell that just by looking at it. Even if it didn't have, as Dr. Veasy records here, 'a heart that is incompatible with life,' first one thing and then another will go wrong with it—its mind, its liver, its kidneys. None of its organs will function properly. Now you folks have other children—I met your fine son. I suggest you consider them. Do not love and fondle this child and give it the will to live—because if it does—it will be tragic."

"It's our fault!" Mama burst out. "They said we're too old to have a child. Or maybe it's because I caught German measles in the fifth month of the pregnancy when the kids brought it home. There was a *Life* magazine article about it, I read it in Dr. Melcher's waiting room a couple of years back. None of the doctors mentioned that. Or what about my chronic urinary tract infections? Those can't be good for a developing fetus."

"It could have been chemicals in the 'bug goop' I'm exposed to every summer. Maybe it was a combination of things. It's going to be tough telling the kids," Dad scratched his head.

"We won't tell the kids that she has a chromosome deficiency! People blame parents for bringing a defective child into the world. *We will be blamed and judged as it is.* But to tell our children, straight out, that their sister has chromosome problems! Imagine what that would do to Judy and Ellen, due to deliver their babies soon! And the younger kids—they'd always worry about their genes and their ability to produce healthy babies." Mama was adamant.

"All right. That part will be our secret," Dad said, untying his shoes. "What else?"

"Holly will know she's loved." Mama blew her nose with a defiant snort. "She will die knowing that her family loves her. Heavenly Father created her, and He gave her to us as she is. If, by some miracle, Holly leaves the hospital, she won't go to an institution like some people suggest. She will come home, where we will love her and care for her. I don't want her to linger or suffer, but I pray that all our kids will be able to see her and hold her. If they have that chance, they will love her despite her problems."

Mama undressed, sighing gratefully as she pulled her nightgown over her head. As she knelt to pray, she was surprised that Dad knelt next to her. They prayed silently for several minutes, then Mama put her hand over his and prayed out loud: "Dear Lord, please forgive us for anything we may have done wrong to cause these problems for our Holly. I have done things that caused her to be born this way, and I am sorry. We thank thee for the kind doctors and nurses at Primary Children's Hospital. They are caring people who bring comfort to Holly, and to other children and families every day.

"Forgive me for resenting Dr. S. Help him to see that Holly isn't an 'it.' She is our sweet, lovely daughter who we love more than life itself. Please, please: we give this tiny one into thy keeping, only help us that we may do nothing to make her endure more pain. We trust Thee to take her home to heaven when the time is right, but if it is Thy will, let us care for her until then."

Mama blamed herself for Holly's suffering, fully and without question, but guilt did not canker her soul. It entwined with her love of Holly into a solid mass of determination, as tangled and as firm as the roots of a quaking aspen grove. Mama had watched her mother, our "Grandma Rhodie," tenderly care for ailing lambs from the family's flock. She had seen her mother nurture her tiny sister and brother, born prematurely, keeping them warm near the open oven door of a woodstove. She yearned to use such loving skills to mother Holly. As she closed her eyes, she thought of holding Holly the next day, crooning to her and smelling her sweetness.

***

Mama and Dad shrouded the chromosomal aspect of Holly's health issues with protective layers of secrecy to protect their children. However, nothing could erase the reality that Holly had significant anomalies. Dr. S. had suggested that Mama and Dad focus on their healthy brood and let Holly slip into death. He knew medicine, and he knew the futility of Holly's condition, but he didn't know Mama and Dad. Though helplessness and hopelessness seemed like natural reactions, they'd learned to face harrowing experiences with faith in God and a loving, dogged endurance. No matter how many days God granted them Holly, she would be loved.

If the fishermen caught fish, Mama got out the Kodak, as she did for this picture from about 1961 in the farmhouse kitchen. From left to right: (Back) Judy, Jeanne, and Dad; (Front) me, Rex, and Andrea (doing her best to hold her fish like Dad and Rex). The dry farm was a dirty place to live, but it sure was fun.

Rex was probably as good at catching fish as Ernest Hemingway's character, Nick Adams. But even the best fishermen get skunked sometimes, as Rex discovered.

Homework Fish

Friday, April 14, 1967

TETON

The house felt empty with Brenda in charge of Rex, Andrea, and me. Bruce was working, but he came home every evening. One night he brought me a new baseball mitt, and he and Kerry often played catch or 500 with me. Slowly my skills improved. I rewarded them by baking a continuous stream of cookies, replenishing flour, eggs, oatmeal, and raisins on credit at the Teton Merc.

I learned that most people in Teton were different from Bea. Many of them asked about Holly with kindness. Min Briggs brought us Wonder Bread bags filled with tuna and bologna sandwiches, along with potato chips, a special treat. Other women dropped off casseroles or homemade bread or cakes. Teton ladies were good cooks.

Sometimes after school, Bill came over to play with our dog, Patches. Bill had strong arms from wielding his crutches, and he could lob a pinecone farther than the other boys lobbed a football. No matter how far Bill threw a cone, Patches sailed through the air, caught it in his teeth, and dropped it. Patches never fetched a cone back to Bill. That was my job. Bill threw cones, Patches caught them, and I gathered them for another round. They never tired of this game, but I did.

Another neighbor, JaNetta "Nettie" Stewart Rackham, "Grandma Rackham" to us, lived a block away. She was 76, with her gray hair drawn into a bun. Running errands for her was our principal source of income. One day, on the way to the post office to get our mail, Andrea and I knocked on her door.

"I like it when she rolls a quarter out of the Alka Seltzer bottle to pay us," Andrea said, knocking on the door. "Let's get penny candy from the Merc."

"Come in!" Grandma shouted.

"Would you like us to get your mail?" I asked.

"Oh, I'm sorry. My daughter brought the mail this morning. And snickerdoodles. Would you like some? How's your Mama and the new baby?"

She offered us a plateful of cookies and poured glasses of milk.

"Holly's about the same as yesterday when you called,

I guess," I mumbled through a mouthful of cookie.

"We'll get the mail tomorrow," I whispered to Andrea.

"Tell us a story about the Depressing, Grandma," Andrea asked. We settled onto the afghan-covered daybed.

"All right. During the Depression, poor men who couldn't find work rode freight trains to Sugar City. They'd walk five miles here to get a meal because some hobo had marked our fence. We fed everybody. Cloe brought all kinds of folks home for supper—once he brought the governor of Idaho. I opened my canned peaches for dessert, and the governor said they were the best by test."

"Tell us more," Andrea begged.

Before the cookies were half gone, she had told us that her mother had died when she was thirteen, leaving her to care for four younger siblings. One day she pushed her toddler brother uptown in the buggy to watch a medicine show, and a handsome young man—Claude "Cloe" Rackham—kept looking at her and offered to push the buggy home. They were married when she was sixteen, and he was twenty.

"We took up a homestead way out on Moody Creek. We were young fools when our first child was born. It took all summer to save enough money to order flannel for diapers and a few baby clothes from the Montgomery Ward catalog. In late October, we got word that our package had arrived in Sugar City, and Cloe went to get it.

"I started to think that this might be the day. I didn't know what was happening, and I felt miserable. I walked a mile to Cloe's mother's place, but I was too scared to ask her for help. All I could think to do was turn around and walk home. Boy, did I hope that Cloe would be there!"

I gaped. Grandma was four years older than me when this happened—Brenda's age! "What did you do, Grandma? Did Cloe come and take you to the hospital?"

"Oh, land, child, there were no hospitals. None of my five children was born in a hospital—they were all born at home."

"So wh—what did you do?"

"Well, I said lots of prayers and went to bed. Things happened. After a while, my sweet baby boy was born, and I wrapped him in a blanket. Here came Cloe and his mother, and boy, were they surprised!"

Andrea's hand slid toward the last snickerdoodle, which I wanted, but I was too interested to stop her.

"Were you scared?" I asked.

She looked me in the eyes. "I was terrified. But I was in God's hands. I knew that, and I knew it again when my other three sons and my daughter were born, and with every other baby I delivered. And that includes quite a few of the people walking the streets of Teton today."

"Were you a *doctor*?"

"No, just a midwife, a poor country midwife."

I wanted to ask, "Were any of the babies sick, like

Holly? Did any die?" but Andrea stood, scattering cookie crumbs.

"Grandma, may I play on your piano?" she asked.

"Absolutely. I never play it!" She grinned.

The spell was broken.

"May I use your bathroom?" I asked. I liked her bathroom. Her soap smelled good, and there was a strip of sandpaper and a box of matches for an air freshener. I lit a match every time, even when I didn't need to.

When I came out, Andrea was on her fifth rendition of "Twinkle, Twinkle." Grandma took my hand in her gnarled hands as I brushed past her chair.

"Three died, Debbie."

"Three babies?"

"Yes, two boys and a girl that I delivered. They're buried in the cemetery on the hill. The boys both came too early. The girl couldn't breathe well. She was kind of blue."

My mouth felt like it was stuck shut with peanut butter.

"I learned, though, that it wasn't my fault. Only God knows when we get to be born and when we get to die. And why. He's in charge. I learned that, and it helped."

She squeezed my hand.

***

Friday, April 21, 1967

TETON

The U.S. Forest Service office in St. Anthony awarded bugging contracts, but Dad hadn't submitted bids. He had decided to work for the Forest Service and other contractors so he could spend more time at home. Dad was working, and motel rooms were expensive, so Holly only saw her family on weekends. After school, Dad, Mama, Shanan, and Brenda headed to Salt Lake City, planning to leave Shanan at Judy's in Fort Hall. Dad said this might be the only time Brenda would see Holly.

Andrea and I curled up on the couch to watch TV. After *Gunsmoke,* I dragged into the kitchen, not eager to cook. Mama said making biscuits was like making cookies, but my biscuits were nowhere near as good as my cookies.

The back door slammed.

"Here's supper," Rex announced, tossing three rainbow trout into the kitchen sink.

"I like fish, but the bones are hard to get out. Yuck, you didn't clean them!"

"Fish is brain food, and *you* could use more of that.

I'll clean them, it's too cold to do that outside like Dad and I usually do. You can cook 'em, though."

"Mama told me to make biscuits to go with ham that's in the fridge," I whined. "I never fried a fish, and I don't want to start now." Rex wasn't going to force me to do any more work than I had to.

He sighed. "Okay, I'll fry 'em. They're *homework fish,*" he said, grabbing a knife.

"Homework fish?" I asked.

"Yeah. Mrs. May made us read *Big Two-Hearted River* by Ernest Hemingway. It's about this guy who goes fishing. She said to read it and answer questions, but Tiny and me said, 'Forget that—we'll fish our own river, then answer the questions.'"

He spread newspaper across the counter, and in a news anchor's voice, announced: "Rex Hemingway here with his newest fish story. Tiny and me went down to the big bend and cast into the pool under the ledge. We caught a few snags in a downed willow tree near the bank. One was so bad I left hook, line, and sinker hanging in the willow."

"That's not news. It happens every time you fish."

"We moved to a different hole, and Tiny caught two small ones. I was getting skunked. Tiny cast further out and caught this guy." He showed Andrea and me the biggest fish, then slit it down the middle, ran a thumb down its spine and spilled its guts onto the newspaper.

"Yucky, gross!" Andrea yelled.

He waved bloody hands at her, and she ran out of the room.

I poured milk into the biscuit dough. The mixture was sluggish, so I added more.

"How did we fry those fish at Scout Camp?" Rex frowned. "Deb, heat some bacon grease in the cast iron frying pan, will ya? Where was I? Tiny gave me these fish—nobody at their house likes fish, which is crazy! So, Tiny asked me, 'What's the best way to catch a fish?' I had nothing—I wasn't catching any. I said, 'I dunno, with trout flies? Or grasshoppers?' And Tiny did this."

Rex turned from the sink and yelled, "*Have somebody throw it at you.*"

He lobbed the fish at me. The slimy thing hit my arm.

The Teton River wound around our lives—boiling over rapids near the farm, where Bruce and these Nelson cousins fished at the Big Hole—and undulating slowly past Teton, where I got in trouble trying to rescue a tree on the river's bank.

Tree-Hugging Gone Wrong

"You're supposed to *catch* the fish, dummy," Rex laughed.

"Catch this!" I threw the fish at his head. He dodged, and it landed in the sink. He threw it at me again, and I tossed it back.

"I'm catching fish right and left!" he yelled.

We threw that fish until we collapsed onto the floor, gasping with laughter.

"Hey, the grease is smoking!" Rex rinsed our flying fish. It sizzled like crazy in the pan.

The ham and Mama's home-canned green beans turned out all right, and Bruce boned the two least-burned fish.

"These biscuits would make good hockey pucks,"

Bruce mumbled, sawing at one with a butter knife.

"Ack, ack, ugh, I swallowed a fishbone!" Andrea gasped, holding her throat.

"Drink water!" Rex offered his glass.

"No, she needs a biscuit! Bread will cover the bone, so it doesn't poke her throat," Bruce yelled, shoving a biscuit at her.

She coughed and waved them away. Then she looked down and stopped coughing. "Oh, look, here's the bone. On my plate!"

***

I looked over Rex's shoulder as he worked on his homework:

1. The story is about World War I and Nick's trauma. So why did Hemingway write about camping and fishing? *War is hell, but fishing and camping are fun.*
2. What do we learn about Nick from the story? *Nick baited his hook with grasshoppers. He was smart.*
3. What did Nick seek in the waters of the big two-hearted river? *Supper.*

***

Saturday, April 22, 1967

TETON

Housework, laundry, and meals slid into chaos. If Mama had been here, she would have made us sweep, mop, and wax the linoleum floors, clean off and dust the desk and table, and maybe even clean our bedrooms. She called it "our Saturday's work."

Mama was not here. We watched cartoons on TV.

Andrea giggled as Yogi Bear tumbled head over heels down a mountain in Jellystone Park.

"I'll save you!" shouted Boo-Boo, holding out a branch.

"Thanks, buddy, you're smarter than the ave-er-age bear!" said Yogi. He pulled hard, and they tumbled down the mountain, splashed into a river, swam to a log, and floated away from Ranger Smith.

Rex dumped a load of firewood next to the stove. He didn't have Saturday's work—he milked the cow twice a day, every day, and chopped wood for our wood-burning stove. "I'm going to the sand dunes with Tiny and Dennis. I'll bank the fire good, so it won't go out on you."

"Stay tuned for our next program, *The Three Stooges Visit the Sahara*," I quipped. "Get your coat, Andi, let's go look at the river. It's no fun being cooped up in here." We put on coats and gloves and went outside.

It was cold, but, thankfully, the snow had melted.

"C'mon, Patches, here boy!" Andrea called. Patches' feathery tail waved as he trotted next to us, crossing the millrace bridge and Briggs's field. The willow trees were turning a color Dad called *gosling gray*. Spring was here!

The full force of the Teton River's spring runoff chewed at a curved bluff. Rainfall and erosion had gnawed at the roots of a small willow tree covered with green buds until it tipped outward near the top of the cliff. It was a short distance from the water's edge, but I thought the churning water might eventually gobble up the earth around the tree and destroy it.

No living thing that survived an Eastern Idaho winter should have to die. Not in the spring. Not this tree with buds like flowers. I could salvage this small tree.

It seemed like Mama, Dad, and my older siblings had whispered, "Holly is going to die. Sometimes God's creations have things go wrong, like Holly's enlarged heart. There's nothing we can do. We're powerless."

I have no power to change things for Holly, and I have no power at school. But I can do something for this little tree.

"We should save that tree. We can pull it up, can't we, Andi? A good tug should bring it upright again." I had no idea what we'd do with it after we straightened it.

"Um, no, let's not." Andrea's wide eyes were on the swollen river.

"You're such a baby."

I grabbed the tree—no movement. I pulled harder. Dirt around my feet gave way and sifted downward, pulling the trunk, branches, and me toward the cold, dark, swift-running current. I landed at the bottom of the bluff, several feet from the water, clutching the tree's limbs.

Andrea was terrified, but at least she was safe. Patches stood protectively by her side. But I couldn't count on help from him. He was no Lassie, the heroic collie on television who saved childrens' lives by running to an adult and barking. Nor did Andrea have a branch like Boo-Boo Bear, which was probably lucky for both of us. The Teton River, roaring behind me, was no cartoon.

In front of me, dirt cascaded down the eroded bluff that had collapsed and gotten me into this mess: standing on a strip of mud just higher than the current.

I had gotten myself into the mess.

Why had I tried to save a stupid tree?

Why had I taken Andrea on this walk?

Wasn't it bad enough that Mama and Dad might have their baby daughter die, and soon?

If I didn't make it up that bank, Bert Briggs would call Primary Children's Hospital and say, "Joyce, Wayne—Debbie got into a fix down at the river. She and Andrea walked there, and she ended up..."

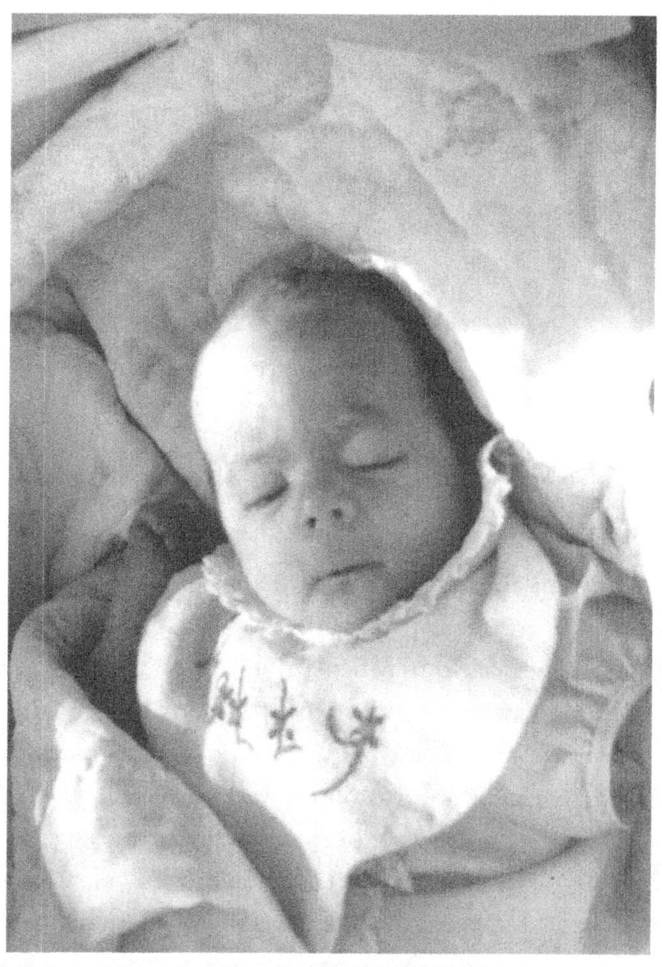

Holly's bib was embroidered by Ellen. Mama and Holly's sisters and aunts sewed and embroidered several articles of clothing for her.

Holly's Homecoming

I was on solid ground, but soil gave way and sifted toward the river when I tried to climb. The tree tipped horizontally, looser than ever. I'd injured my sternum, and it hurt when I tried to scramble up the steep slope without sliding toward the river.

Andrea looked heavenward, and her voice rose with every word: "Dear Father in Heaven, please help Debbie get away from the water! Daddy and Mama need to be with Holly. Please don't let Debbie drown." Her voice reached a frantic wail as she wiped her nose on her coat sleeve, "Cause they're worried enough already!"

I made myself take a deep breath. *Would more dirt slide away? Would the river eat up the ground beneath me?*

"Dammit!" I yelled. Dad would've said that, and it should make me feel better. It didn't.

I could hear Bert's sorrowful voice, "She ended up ... trapped near the water; we got her out." Or "trapped several hours ... hypothermia ... " Or "Andrea came and got me, but... Debbie drowned."

Patches whined. I looked over my shoulder. An uprooted cottonwood tree twisted toward me in the current, seeking quiet eddies in which to rest, but dragged relentlessly back into the fast-moving water. That could be me.

My eyes prickled. *What a dope! I'm in charge. Dad, Mama, and Brenda are gone, and Rex doesn't know where we are. What if I can't get back up the bank? Will more dirt slide away and wash me into the river? Will I drown?* I stared at the swift-moving tree.

"Honey!" Andrea called. The sunshine blazed behind her, lighting up her dark-blond hair. Her voice was firm.

"Honey, get out of there!"

She never called me honey, but Mama did. Mama! In Salt Lake City, worrying about Holly. I looked at the madly boiling water filled past its brim with debris.

"Don't look at the water!" Andrea commanded.

I took a deep breath. She was right. The river wasn't going to suck me in if I didn't let it. Dad said, "Use the good sense God gave you." I needed to think this out. *What are my choices? To my left, the bluff is sheer and high.*

To my right, it is lower, but the willow tree leans out crazily over the river. I better not tug at those loose roots again. Last year's weeds and grasses were rooted in the middle, halfway up the steep bluff. *I've put on weight this year. Mama says I'm "becoming a teenager." Can those weeds hold me?* I grasped a handful and tugged. They held. I pulled myself up a short way. One handful of weeds tore out of the ground, but I quickly grabbed another. It held. Step by step, one bunch of weeds after another, I crawled up the bluff.

At the top, I flopped on the ground.

Throwing her arms around me, Andrea whispered, "God answers prayers, doesn't He?"

"He does. Thanks for your prayer and for what you told me to do. God helped you to help me."

Patches licked my face. "Okay, okay, I love you too, you crazy dog." We started across Briggs's field.

"One more thing," I said, my face turning red. "I won't tell Mama or Dad because they'd be worried. You shouldn't tell them either, okay?"

Andrea nodded slowly. "I won't. And I'm never going to try to rescue a tree. Ever."

Diary, Saturday, April 22, 1967: Andi and I [were] taking [a]walk on river. Dirt undermined. I fell and hurt my chest bone. Bathed.

***

Wednesday, April 26, 1967

TETON

Mama, Dad, Brenda, and Shanan got home Sunday night. On Tuesday, a doctor from back East examined Holly. He called Mama and told her that Holly would not live long, but she could come home. Dad, Mama, and Bruce drove to Salt Lake City and brought Holly home in the back of the Fairlane.

Medical specialists had done all they could for Holly. Now it was up to us to take care of her.

At 3 p.m., Andrea hurtled out of the schoolhouse.

"Mama's home! I got to go!" she hollered. I had to run hard to catch up.

Dad placed Holly's bassinet in the dining room, away from drafts and near the stove. Mama wound Holly's brown hair around her finger to make a curl on top of her head—the only place where Shanan could touch Holly or kiss her.

"Debbie, wash your hands and put on a mask. You can hold her!" Mama smiled at me from the couch, with Andrea jammed tight to her side and Shanan on her lap.

I was scared I might hurt Holly. She was so tiny, and somewhat stiff. *She isn't round and pink-cheeked like*

Andrea, Shanan, and Michael were. Holly's left ear is folded under the skin of her scalp like a tight-closed rosebud. My tears fell. This baby was so different!

Kerry held Holly tenderly and Shanan showed her excitement to have a baby sister. Mama enlisted all older members of the family to teach the little girls to enjoy Holly without holding her.

Happy Together

Mama smiled at me. "We'll get used to her," she whispered.

Holly's stillness stilled me. I relaxed.

Shanan slipped up next to me. "Her makes butterfly breaths," she whispered.

I'd known Holly from the descriptions of those who had seen her. Now, I held her. Her face was pinched, and when she opened her eyes, one wandered or crossed. I'd prayed for her, and now I loved her. For 20 days, we had worried that Holly would die in Salt Lake City—now, here she was, tiny and sweet. She was home!

Mama didn't let us, or herself, get our hopes too high. She said Holly would only stay with us for a few days, perhaps thinking that she wouldn't have the skills to care for this fragile infant who had been spirited away so soon after birth. She didn't say Holly might return to the hospital. Or that Holly might die soon. But she thought it.

Mama had used many tools while raising nine healthy children—singing and breast milk, baby powder and clean diapers, and lots of love, passing the baby around to siblings who were taught to be gentle. Many of these methods were denied to Holly because of her condition. And she needed so much more.

Would Mama know what to do? Would we be able to help?

One thing was sure: when Holly was in the hospital, Mama and Daddy were gripped by crushing helplessness because they were either far away, or not in control of her care. Now they were in charge. They knew how to love kids, and maybe that would be enough for Holly.

Diary, Wednesday, April 26, 1967: Holly's home! She is beautiful and so very small. I have to wear an oxygen mask because of my head cold.

Brenda was feeding Holly formula with an eyedropper under Mama's watchful eye a few days later. When the baby cried fretfully—not loudly, but persistently—Brenda whispered to me, "Shanan never fussed like this. Mama fed her, or we rocked her, and she settled." We looked at each other sadly—how could we listen to a baby cry and not be able to help her?

Mama heard us. She knew what we were thinking.

"It's all right, girls. Doctor Veasy said crying strengthens her lungs." Her voice trembled a little. "Breathing takes most of her strength. Holly has a weak sucking reflex, so give her a very little at a time. You're good with that eyedropper, Brenda." She smiled. "Holly is doing her tiny best to stay alive. If we do our best, Holly will sense our love."

Mama and Dad had not forgotten that Judy would soon have her baby. We faithfully walked to the post office to mail their letters to her.

LETTER FROM JOYCE NELSON TO JUDY HIDALGO

May 10, '67

Teton

Dear First-born,

We're surely wondering about you and just praying all will go well down there.

So many things come to my mind that I want to say to you, but by the time there is time to jot them down, I've forgotten.

The miracle of life is so close to us now.

Holly seems fine today; her Daddy says, "pink as a flower" and this is amazing since she had a bad night. We've had her on oxygen now for (well, since the next night after you left). With it she is so good, sleeps and breathes so good. We'd prayed for something to ease any suffering and I guess this is our answer. (When Heavenly Father wants her, he can take her, we know, in spite of all our poor powers, so we feel really good about the oxygen.) She looks at all of us and seems to enjoy being held so much. We give her pan baths now and she surely relaxes and rests better, and how Shan, Andy and Deb enjoy her baths!

I must go change her now. Jeanne and Alan coming Thursday evening May 11. Love you and hope you make it to the hospital in plenty of time, we will call maybe before this gets there to check on you.

Love,

Mom

This little article, read and know this is how we felt (and how you did about Michael and will again this time). And will you save it for El? [Enclosure was lost.]

LETTER FROM WAYNE NELSON TO JUDY HIDALGO

We brought Holly home April 25. She weighed 5 lb. 6 oz. Since, she has gained another 4 oz. On May 4 we checked with our Dr. (second time) and when we got home had to put her under oxygen again. She had been without oxygen for ten days. Last week she had a lot of colic so we added ten drops of paregoric and a little sugar to her water. Then she would take a lot of water but very little formula, so I added the paregoric to the formula. She really snapped

out of it, got pink as an apple blossom and really looked good. Today she seems to tire easily and is more listless. [Other pages of this letter have been lost.]

Holly would spend the next three months with an oxygen tank next to her bassinet and an oxygen tube next to her nose. Once again, Dad's knowledge and skill at using oxygen for welding made Holly's care easier for us than it would have been for other families.

***

Monday, May 1, 1967

HOG HOLLER

Brenda jammed the pickup gas pedal to the floor, cranking the radio to "Little Deuce Coupe," taking us away from home, away from the demands of our big family. Away from one tiny, helpless soul.

Hog Holler, a green valley intersected by serpentine windings of the Teton River, was too pretty for its name. I asked, "Did hogs live here?"

"They did and were in hog heaven."

We scrambled up a bank where a waterfall cascaded over lava rock. A shaft of precious sunlight prismed the mist into a rainbow, and I could no longer swallow the lump in my throat.

"I miss Mama and Daddy." I wasn't sure what I was trying to say, but if anyone could understand, it'd be Brenda.

"Yeah, me too."

"Mama's always, um, taking care of Holly. She didn't go to church with us yesterday. She can't think of anyone else! Dad doesn't tease us anymore."

Brenda tossed a pebble into the mist.

"I know."

Brenda, who usually chattered nonstop to Mama about boys at school or her DJ friend, had been quiet lately. "If one of us was sick, they'd do the same for us."

I nodded.

"We have to get through it. Mama and Dad love us—that hasn't changed. Holly needs us—all of us, though not as much as she needs Mama. You've been working hard, helping around the house."

Wow! She noticed! I'd been trying. We were a messy bunch, and it was frustrating because all the work had to be done again after the next meal or on the next day.

"You, too, sis," I mumbled. "You did all the laundry and made stew yesterday. You haven't been calling your DJ."

"He's not *my* DJ!" She laughed. "We have to work harder, but it doesn't mean we can't have fun. It doesn't mean we have to quit living our lives."

"Our *LOVE lives*?" I grinned.

"You bet!—especially our love lives! Hey, Angells live

a few miles from here. Those boys are cute—all of them cowboys, riding their Dad's rodeo stock. But they're short!" Brenda was six feet tall and hoped to find a man at least the same height. One of the Angell boys was in her class, and they were friends.

It was too windy to slip through the mist to the cave behind the falls like we would've done in summer, so we got back into the truck.

"Want to drive past Angells and see the bronc rider from my class?"

"Nah. He's old. At least 16—no short, old angels for me!" My toes were cold, sticking out of the holes in my Keds.

"Look at those whitetails." She took her hand off the key, and we watched a herd of deer sniff the air and slide into the willows.

Brenda cranked the truck into a U-turn. "We're luckier than Mama. We can get in this truck and take a ride anytime." She gunned the engine. "Let's go frost Ellen and Kerry's birthday cake!" The Turtles sang about the weather and being happy together as dark clouds crowded in from the north.

Brenda's favorite disc jockey came on: "It's a chilly Mayday at 30°F! Our mean daily temperature has been 38°F for two weeks."

"That *IS* mean!" Brenda yelled.

It was a bona fide Idaho spring. Snow fell that night.

***

Friday, May 12, 1967

TETON

I wrote one or two sentences about Holly in my diary every night. Here are a few from early May:

"I helped feed Holly ... She is healthier ... Helped feed & take care of Holly ... Holly is getting worse ... She went to the doctor ... Dad brought home two oxygen tanks for her ...Holly worse, still has oxygen ... Holly is better than before ... She eats an ounce in a feeding ... I played and took care of Holly ... Holly is reacting to love beautifully ... Holly had fairly bad day ... Holly same ... Holly went to Doc ... She lost weight ... Holly perkier."

At school, I thought about Holly, and at lunch, I ran the two blocks home to eat and see how she was doing. Bea had few chances to torment me, but one morning she caught me.

"Hey, Debra, I heard your sister is *re-tarded.*"

"My baby sister has an enlarged heart."

"That makes her *re-tarded.*" A few kids giggled. Wendy and Bill looked miserable. Bill and his mom had visited Holly.

Anger ignited every cell in my body. *Of all the unfair words in this unfair world—I will not let Bea pick on Holly!*

I took five steps, planning to knock Bea down, pull her hair, and punch her face. On the fifth step, I remembered: One of Bea's brothers, a teenager, had died during our fourth-grade year. *Bea hurts ME with words. Why not?*

"Don't you dare talk that way about my sister! Your brother was sick, too. He died—maybe because he'd rather be six feet under in the cemetery than live with you!"

Bea turned pukey-faced, like I'd socked her in the stomach.

Mr. Gee breezed into the room and then stopped, taking in the scene. "Debra and Bea, come to my office. Class, open your social studies books and read chapter twenty-three."

I'd been in his office. But I had never gone because I was in trouble. I dragged myself down the hall, wondering why I didn't feel more like I'd conquered Bea. After all, she was crying this time.

"What happened?" Mr. Gee's brown eyes were steely.

"She … she made fun of my brother who died!" Bea choked out.

"Debra!" He turned to me. "You did?"

"I … I did. I mean, I don't think I *made fun* of her brother, but I said he'd rather be in the cemetery than with Bea." Saying it made me feel miserable. I wished I'd pulled her hair instead.

"Apologize to Bea. We show respect for the dead and for the feelings of their families."

Alan and Jeanne came to see Baby Holly after their school semester ended. Dad or Judy snapped this picture with Mama and Patches in front of the lilac bush in Teton.

Mother's Day With Holly

Mr. Gee was right. It was horrible of me to say that to anyone, even to Bea; maybe especially to Bea, because somehow, I knew how much she had loved her brother. She hadn't been as snotty before he died.

I mumbled an apology. Bea accepted, blowing her nose delicately with two tissues.

"Bea, go back to class and read the social studies assignment," Mr. Gee said. She walked out slowly, without even a flounce in my direction.

Mr. Gee sighed. "Debra, I'll need to call your parents."

"Please, don't. My baby sister is so sick. It would break Mama's heart." Now *I* was sobbing.

"I heard that your sister was in the hospital in Salt

Lake. She's home now, right?" he asked. I nodded.

"Can you tell me what's wrong?" His eyes were kind again.

"She has an enlarged heart, and the doctors say that she may not live very long . . ." I could've stopped there, but I had to ask. I couldn't ask Mama or Dad. "Mr. Gee, what does *retarded* mean? I don't think Holly *is* retarded, but that's what Bea said."

The clock ticked, louder than the one in the classroom during a test. Mr. Gee cleared his throat. "*Retarded* means *delayed.* Some people are born with conditions that slow them down physically or mentally, and that's a label people put on them. I don't like that label, and I will speak to Bea. I understand now why you got angry."

He scratched his head. "I won't call your parents, but don't be cruel to anyone, even Bea. It hurts you more than it hurts the other person."

I nodded. We moved toward the door, then he stopped.

"Bea *will* apologize to you. I'm not blind. This year has been hard for you. Hang on for a few more weeks, and after summer vacation, you'll be in junior high school. It's not a piece of cake, but there are more students. I'm sure you'll find friends."

Wow. I thought nobody but me knew what was going on with me.

***

Andrea spotted Jeanne and Alan's car in front of our house as we walked home. We broke into a run. They were here to meet baby Holly and for Mama, for Mother's Day. Mama was happiest when all her children were gathered around in a crowded, noisy bunch.

Jeanne proudly said that Alan had graduated and now held a bachelor's degree from the University of Idaho. Alan told of their move to Boise, where they would work for the summer transcribing law library records in the Idaho State Capitol Building.

Jeanne taught Andrea and me how to make Popcorn Cake with marshmallows, popcorn, and gumdrops. It was the best dessert we'd ever had.

At 9:32 p.m., Mama said, "Girls, you've had way too much of that cake. Get ready for bed now. Brenda, you and Debbie make up the couch bed in the living room. You girls get everything you need for tomorrow out of the girls' room so Jeanne and Alan can sleep there."

We grumbled, but Brenda curled up on an air mattress on the floor, and Andrea and Shanan fell asleep next to me on the couch bed.

I couldn't sleep on ten inches of mattress, and besides, Mama was talking to Jeanne nearby. Holly fussed, and there was a squirting sound.

"An enema helps her—she can't seem to get it out on her own. Now let's give her a warm bath so she can sleep," Mama said.

"She looks like Grandma Nelson," Jeanne murmured. Ellen said the same thing, and it was true. *Is it because they look like each other? Or because Grandma lost the sight of one eye as a child, and Holly's right eye seems to be nearly closed most of the time?* I wondered, but I never dared ask. Mama was sensitive about Holly's looks.

"Oh, how cute, Mama. You're curling her hair!"

"Some of you kids didn't have enough hair to make a curl."

"Oh yes! Debbie and Shanan!" Jeanne laughed.

"Shanan finally has enough hair so that Brenda can get it around a curler! Doesn't Holly have pretty hair? The nurses at Primary Children's gave her this 'million-dollar hair-do,' and dressed her in a little rosebud dress. They treat the babies so well there." Mama's voice broke. "The little boys on either side of Holly—Lane, and Casey—couldn't live very long."

Jeanne whispered, "I'm sorry. Dad said the nurses and doctors are nice, though."

Mama was quiet. "They're nice. Very kind, and very smart. They know there's not much they can do…." She fumbled to find a box of tissues but came up with a roll of toilet paper, which Dad kept handy all over the house.

"They are all so good. But that day—the day four doctors told us there was no hope for our baby—one doctor called Holly 'it' and said she would … die. My world was crashing down around my feet. Some nurses near us were laughing and talking about something, about a party. And … my world was crashing."

Mama's shoulders heaved. I squeezed my eyes shut and wished I'd tried harder to sleep.

"Mama. I'm sorry," Jeanne murmured, putting Holly's nighty on.

"They were good to us; they took good care of her. They couldn't help it that they couldn't tell us what we so much wanted to hear: that there was something they could DO for her. I appreciate them. And I'm glad we did our best to get her to good doctors—we didn't give up and let her die." Mama blew her nose.

Jeanne held Mama—who was holding Holly—for the longest time, long after I slept.

Jeanne held both Holly and Timothy, Judy and Silver Hidalgo's new baby boy, in front of Mama's beloved French lilac bush.

Running from the Bus in Nylons with Runners

May 15, 1967

TETON

Dr. Melcher suggested that Mama use a "preemie" nipple on a regular baby bottle. It helped Holly to swallow. So Mama let us feed Holly her bottle sometimes, with the oxygen tube tucked near her nose.

Holly cried from pain that Mama couldn't soothe, and Mama reminded us that it strengthened Holly's lungs. She said it often, but not like she believed it.

Diary, Monday, May 15, 1967: Holly's day was worse. School is all in a rush to get over. I helped Mom. Judy had a baby boy last night. TIMOTHY NELSON HIDALGO!!!

***

Saturday, May 20, 1967

TETON

"Debbie, get ready. You need to look nice. I called the bus station, and you can get a ticket if Brenda gets you to Rexburg pronto."

While Mama cared for Holly, a big piece of her heart was with Judy. So Mama had a plan. There would be no cartoons or Saturday's work for me. Mama's talent for delegating had kicked in, and she was sending me to Judy's to help her with her new baby, who we called Timmy.

I put on my paisley suit and my girdle. I hated that girdle, but it both sucked in my gut and held up my nylons with "garters," one in front, and one in the back, on each leg. A garter was a plastic button placed beneath the fabric of the stocking and anchored with a metal clip.

"Brenda, the button on this garter broke off! And of course, the nylons have runners!" I wailed.

"Use a penny to fix your garter. And when did runners ever stop us? Hurry—the bus leaves in thirty-five minutes!" Brenda crammed my pajamas, clothes, and underwear into a grocery bag. I secured my defective nylons with a penny, ran a brush through my hair, and we were off.

On the bus, I whispered what Judy had told me: "*Have the driver go half a mile past the Fort Hall bus stop and let you off at our lane.*"

In Fort Hall, the driver motioned me to get off, but I told him I needed to go further. He scowled.

At Judy's lane, I murmured, "Please. Stop here." He didn't hear me, and barreled ahead, picking up speed. Houses and trees sped by. The lane was behind us.

Where will the bus stop next? Pocatello, in half an hour. I'd have to call Judy—who had had a new baby—to drive to the bigger town to pick me up.

I HAD to make him stop. I cleared my throat. My face burned red. "STOP!" I yelled.

The bus driver swore, hit the brakes, and glared at me. I hurried off the bus amid angry comments from passengers.

As the diesel fumes faded, I trudged down Idaho Highway 191, carrying my paper bag. I was far beyond Judy's lane.

Cars sped by, so I walked in the gutter, scooping weed seeds and pebbles into my church flats. I hadn't had a drink before we left Rexburg. My mouth was dry, and I was hungry.

Spring comes quicker to Fort Hall than to Teton. Sweat made circles under the sleeves of my suit and trickled inside the tight girdle. When I tugged at it, the penny pinged into the gravel and my nylon stocking sagged below the hem of my skirt.

Cars slowed as they passed. I was sure that the people in them were giving me funny looks. A large truck zoomed by, and I jumped further into the barrow pit, snagging my nylons on dry weeds.

What a relief to finally turn onto Judy's lane, plod down it, and knock on her door!

Baby Timmy was a delight—so healthy, so strong, as he wailed loudly and nursed hungrily at Judy's breast. Not like Holly.

I changed clothes, read to Michael, and played with him outside before Judy and I fixed supper. I wasn't as much help as Mama would have been.

The next day Silver and Judy drove me home, and I wrote in my diary, *Holly & Timmy sure look cute together.*

We played with cousins in our camper bus wherever it was parked. Left to right: Roger Keller, Gary Furniss, Shanan, Marilyn Furniss, me, and Andrea, with Susan Keller in front, and a couple of unknown dogs. Photo taken during a break from playing in the bus parked in the driveway at Teton in 1969.

Best Cousins, Best Friends

Thursday, May 25, 1967

TETON AND CLEMENTSVILLE

My cousin Marilyn was my best friend. Sure, she was my only friend, but she would've been best no matter what. It was a sweet surprise when she ran toward Andrea and me after school, shouting, "I'm spending the afternoon with you guys while Mom runs to Rexburg!"

Marilyn and I were about the same height. She had dark brown naturally curly hair, while mine was lighter and straight. She loved kittens and cats, and I tolerated them. She had five older brothers and sisters and one younger brother, and I had six older siblings and three younger sisters. When we drowned in seas of bossy, annoying siblings, we turned to each other, held on, and were as silly or dreamy or emotional as we needed to be. We were each other's life preservers.

Dad walked in as we gobbled a snack.

"I need to plow the garden at the farm before we move up there. If you girls want to come, jump in the pickup!" he said.

In minutes, Dad, Marilyn, and I rumbled up Highway 33 toward Clementsville, Idaho. It wasn't a ghost town. It was a ghost community. When Dad grew up there, a tight-knit group of farmers spread over many miles, many of them living in the shallow canyons that skirted the Big Hole Mountains. Farming had changed, and like us, many had sold their acreages.

"Are you guys rich? You have two houses!" Marilyn said.

Dad laughed. "Honey, we barely have enough money to get by. We rent the house in Teton, but when we sold our farmland, we kept the house and a piece of the canyon. It's useless range land, but we move there in summer to graze our cow and grow the garden."

Brenda had told me that to Dad this place that we called "the farm" symbolized his failure at dry farming, but because Mama loved the trees, sky, wildflowers, and chislers (Uinta ground squirrels), Dad moved us there every summer as he had during the farming years. Mama said there was no better place to teach us kids to work by growing a vegetable garden, raising a pig, and milking our cow, Swiss Miss. We worked and played with Nelson cousins and local kids in the Clementsville 4-H Club managed by our aunt, Seville Nelson.

Plowing the garden was the first step in our spring move to the farm. When Dad turned off the ignition, Marilyn and I ran into the house. Instead of the usual closed-house, slightly mousy smell we expected, we were hit with the stench of rotting venison, beef, vegetables, huckleberries, and orange juice. Dad peeked into the International Harvester chest freezer in the enclosed front porch.

"Whew!" He slammed the lid. "It was fine two weeks ago." He flipped the light switch. Nothing. "Power went off. Somebody's going to have to clean this up!"

He looked at us.

"No, Dad!"

He ignored me. "You won't have water—the power to the well pump is off. I've got to plow."

And he was gone.

"We are not going to clean that! We're not!" I yelled when Dad was out of earshot.

Marilyn ran from the choking odor of the freezer to the big swing that Dad had built, its chains suspended from a crossbeam atop two lodgepole pine poles that stood twenty-five feet high. Marilyn stood on the wide seat and started pumping.

"I hate it! Making us clean up that poopy stuff!" I

yelled. Mama, who didn't like us using bathroom words, would've been shocked. Marilyn was shocked but rose to the challenge: "It stinks like a cowboy outhouse after a hot bean chili feed!" She broke into song: "Beans, beans, the musical fruit, the more you eat, the more you toot!"

She pumped the swing high, high, high enough to see the top of the opposite hill and north to the plains beyond our canyon. Almost to Ashton, forty miles away. She slowed the swing and bailed out. I took my turn at swinging and singing about beans, until I had a thought: "Let's go see if Timothy Creek is running!"

When Dad turned the tractor away from us, we ran along the canyon floor, moist and rich with grass.

"Why do you guys call it Timothy Creek?" Marilyn asked.

"When Brenda was little, she saw the trickle of water that runs down our canyon every spring when the snow-drifts melt. She asked Dad why our canyon doesn't have a creek, like Pony Creek, Canyon Creek, and Crooked Creek. Dad said she could name our creek, and that's what she named it."

"Did Judy name her baby after it?"

"I dunno. Look, the snow is all melted, so the creek dried up, like it does every year." We picked the first wildflowers of spring: sweet Virginia bluebells and tiny yellow Johnny-jump-ups, then Marilyn turned toward the house. "You know we've got to do it."

I groaned. "Okay."

We sucked in the herbal scent of aspen, sagebrush, and mud to fortify our nostrils against the stench that would assail us in the front porch.

The big swing Dad built could be pumped by three kids at once: Rex, me, Junior Wright, and Andrea (holding on for dear life). After swinging, we would jump off and race down the dugway road to the left (1962).

Our Work Stinks

I opened the freezer and gagged. "This is baaaad!" My eyes watered.

"Don't be a baby." Marilyn found two plastic bowls in the kitchen. "We'll dip stuff up in these. Where will we dump them?"

The swill bucket—which we filled with food scraps to feed the pig when we lived at the farm—was in the yard, half-filled with mud and snowmelt. We dumped it and carried it to the front porch.

We scooped up putrid packages of meat, floating bags of bread, the most pungent huckleberries anyone ever experienced, a whole chicken that disintegrated at a touch, nasty beans, peas, and corn, rotten broths from soup, spoiled raspberries, sour chokecherry juice, and pulpy cardboard containers of orange juice concentrate. It all went into the swill bucket, which we carried time after time into thickets of brush and aspen trees far from the house. Mice, chipmunks, and coyotes, as well as good old bacteria, would gobble up the rotten food.

We wiped the freezer with dry rags and propped it open as Dad honked the signal that he was ready to head home.

As we settled into the truck, Dad said, "Whew! What a st—" I shot him a dirty look, and he clamped his mouth shut, rolling his window down.

The swill bucket had reminded me of something, and I asked, "Dad, are you buying a pig this summer?"

"Hadn't thought of it." He passed his hand over his crew-cut, thinking. "Pork on the hoof is kind of high. And Mama needs you to help with Holly. I guess not."

"Yippee!" I squealed.

"What?" Dad laughed. "You mean you won't miss home-cured bacon, Canadian bacon, and hams, and sausage, pork chops and roasts, and lard for pies?"

"I'll miss those, for sure! But I won't miss feeding a pig!"

I had broken both arms, and both healed crookedly, before I turned eight. Mama often reminded me: "Dr. Melcher said carrying heavy weights straightens the bones of your arms." For years, my daily summer job had been to carry the swill bucket and a bucket of water from the well to the pig in the barn—about one hundred yards. Now, Dad had granted me a reprieve from pig work!

When we walked into the house, Shanan wrinkled her nose. "You guys 'TINK!!" she shouted.

Marilyn had a quick bath and put on some of my clothes before going home, and I had a long soaky bath in the claw-footed tub. As I submerged into suds, I murmured, "Cleaning that freezer was the most heroic grown-up job we've ever done!"

***

Friday, May 26, 1967

TETON AND CLEMENTSVILLE

I survived! School's out! I thought, time and again, on the last day of school. I even smiled at Bea.

"Why are you so happy?" she snarled. She'd avoided me for three weeks after she had mumbled an apology just loud enough for Mr. Gee to hear.

Why? I'm free of Bea and her gang for the next three months! Andrea and I ran all the way home, as liberated as the killdeer who cried shrilly when they heard us coming.

"Mama, it's over! I'm a seventh grader!" I yelled as we busted into the house.

"Did you make 'last-day-of-school-cookies' like last year?" Andrea shouted, throwing her arms around Mama's waist.

"Hush, girls, hush. Holly is having troubles," Mama said. Holly lay on a towel on the table, crying her faint cry, and Mama held the ear syringe—an enema. Gag.

"C'mon, Andi. I'll cut some bread. Maybe there's jam." Tears of self-pity dripped on the bread knife and on my crooked slices of homemade bread. Mama had hardly looked at us. Day after day after day, Mama was too busy or too tired for us, but not for every little thing that Holly needed—which she needed all day and all night.

Andrea called her friend, Jocelyn. Lucky Andrea—to have a friend around the corner. They'd play Barbies the rest of the day.

"Mama!" Dad was as loud as us kids when he came in the door. "I've got a load for the farm. I'm heading up there." He walked to the table and brushed a finger across the top of Holly's head.

"Oh, good. Take Debbie. She can scrub out that freezer and mop the floors. Debbie, get a couple of jugs of hot water, soap, bleach, and rags. Load your clothes into boxes and throw them in the truck. And as many of Andrea's as you can."

She's sticking me with that putrid freezer again! Without Marilyn around to help or make it fun!

Dad could tell I was sulky, so he whistled for Patches. Maybe there'd be time for me to throw sticks for the dog, even though Patches didn't fetch sticks any better than he did pinecones.

We barreled down the highway in the old pickup

truck. Patches stuck his head into the wind, and Dad laughed. "His eyeballs are going to dry out."

When we rumbled over Canyon Creek bridge, I looked at the tall pine trees whose roots drank the churning water of the creek bed at the bottom of the canyon. It made me dizzy, but I did it every time. The fields were turning soft green, yielding the scent of rain. Uncle Henry and Uncle Lester would have a good harvest of winter wheat. *I'm free from school for three months. What the heck, I feel good, even if I do have to clean the freezer!*

Rain had pounded the dirt road all night, and Dad did some fancy driving to keep from getting stuck in mud holes. When we arrived, I nearly stepped on a long black garter snake stretched across the warm cement of the steps.

"Whoa, Dad! She scared me!" I gently touched the snake's smooth scales as she slithered into a crack. Patches sniffed the place she had lain.

"She's our friend!" Dad said. "Keeping the mouse population under control." Our weird family welcomed a garter snake to the basement to live a hidden, rodent-rich life.

We unloaded clothes and cleaning supplies, and Dad replaced fuses in the fuse box, then drove to the shop. Scrubbing the freezer with warm, bleachy water was easier than emptying it had been. I plugged it in to get cold.

Mama said to sweep and mop, but I've done enough. I

nearly ran to the swing, but then I remembered Holly. We couldn't bring her to a place with filthy floors. I dragged out the broom, mop and bleach, and an hour later the floors were clean.

A wild howl rent the air, curdling my blood. I ran toward Patches' strangled yelps.

Has a coyote attacked the dog in broad daylight?

Patches dug at his face with his paws. His nose and jowls were peppered with long quills. In the shade of the barn lay a dead porcupine, looking like she might get up and waddle away, blond quills bobbing. Dad strode up the hill.

"Get the needle-nose pliers, Deb." Dad grunted as he sat on the ground. "That old mama pegged out a day or two ago. Come here, boy."

He cradled Patches' head in his left arm, but Patches, frantic with pain, wiggled away.

"Get him, Deb!"

Patches joined every photograph taken outdoors, like this one in the orchard at Teton in 1963. Lucky for him, Andrea, age four, and Dad agreed that he was the sweet center of the Nelson family's universe.

Patches, What Can We Do?

I ran after Patches. Usually, he'd be far ahead of me, but he stopped to paw at the quills burning his sensitive nose and face. I dragged him to Dad.

"C'mon, boy. C'mere, it's all right." Dad crooned. "You had to sniff that stinky old thing, didn't you? Maybe more than once? Deb, I've got his head, hold his hind-quarters still."

Patches squirmed, especially when Dad got a good grip on a quill and jerked it out. It was hard to hold him, especially with Dad advising me and cussing Patches, even while muttering sweet words to him. Patches was a medium-sized dog, white with brown patches, with a beautiful, plumed tail.

Patches got away once, wrenching free with a

heart-rending yowl, but he didn't run far. His dog wisdom told him that although Dad was hurting him, the quills had to come out, and he needed to endure the pain.

Dad found a rhythm, and Patches—good dog that he was—held still. I didn't want to be there, holding Patches down, hearing him whine, and seeing the suffering in his sweet eyes. I glanced at the porcupine mama and thought that she would never again parade along with a litter of little ones behind her, reminding us that she owned this place through squatter's rights and the sting of her quills.

Patches jerked as Dad removed a quill near his nose. Silent tears coursed down Dad's face; his nose was running, and he swiped it across his shoulder. I'd never seen Dad cry. Fifteen quills littered the damp ground.

"I'm sorry, boy. So sorry," he murmured. "A bad break. You're a good boy; you never deserved this. Nobody deserves to suffer."

He was talking to Patches, and he meant every word. Yet he was also talking to—who?

My mouth opened, and what came out surprised me.

"Dad! Mama says, every day, that Holly is better, or maybe worse, or something. When she was born you said she might die. But she hasn't. Will she?" I choked, "Will she grow up, or not?"

Dad looked at me, then at the three quills piercing Patches' face. He picked up the rhythm. When the last quill lay on the ground, we let Patches go to whine and quiver out his pain.

Dad stood. "Debbie, the best doctors we could find say Holly has a lot wrong with her. Her heart is enlarged, and kidney problems go with that." He tossed the pliers into the toolbox. "Honey, she'll die. We don't know when."

He pulled out his bandana, wiped his face, blew his nose, and opened his arms. I closed my eyes and memorized Dad's hug: his smell—Camel cigarettes and sweat; the feel of his shoulder, soaked with tears and snot; the security of his arms and his willingness to hang on for a long time. I patted his back like he was a baby, and he didn't budge.

Dad, and especially Mama, took care of Holly all day and all night. But they didn't want their other children to feel unneeded or unloved. They made sure we were not hungry, cold, or without clothes. They served us as staunchly as they did her, but differently. Holly's suffering had broken our family's hearts over the past two months, yet when we cuddled her frail body, fed her, changed her, or helped with the necessary work of our big family—including holding a suffering dog—we were made whole.

***

Saturday, May 27, 1967

TETON AND CLEMENTSVILLE

We moved twice a year—in May, to the farmhouse, and in September, back to the Teton house that sat empty during the summer. Dad and his moving crew—sometimes his sons, heaven help us if it was Mama and his daughters—loaded furniture into the old farm truck for the eighteen-mile trip. Though Mama swaddled it all with quilts and blankets, it got banged up. Dad often said, "Seven moves is as good as a fire."

Lucky for us, Bruce and Rex helped this time, moving the furniture in two trips. Dad hurried them along, loading and unloading, backing the truck bed up to the front steps of both houses. The air turned blue from cussing when they negotiated the narrow stairs up to the boys' and girls' bedrooms at the farmhouse.

Mama and the girls hauled pots and pans, bedding, house plants, food, clothing, and books, including the World Book Encyclopedias, which provided the final say in many an argument, and offered us research and entertainment. Mama and Dad couldn't afford many things, but Mama was proud that she had arranged for time payments with the traveling encyclopedia salesman to buy our World Books before Teton Elementary School purchased a set.

All day, Mama and Brenda alternated staying with Holly in the quiet Teton house and driving loads to the farm in the car. In the evening, Dad stopped in Teton to say goodbye; moving had put him behind the rest of his boss's bugging crew. Bruce and Rex left from the farm to join their crew, working in a different area.

We loaded the trunk. Brenda slid into the driver's seat, Andrea squeezed in next to her, and I held Shanan on my lap. Mama sat with Holly and her bassinet in the back seat, along with the oxygen tank and its plastic tube at Holly's nostrils.

Four minutes out, Shanan piped up, "I need to go potty!"

"Hang on, honey. We'll be there soon!" Mama soothed. "I'll tell you the story of Peter Rabbit!" Mama dragged it out, adding extra adventures with Mr. McGregor. Shanan wiggled but listened. We were bumping up the dirt road to the house before Peter was finally sent to bed.

"The farmhouse looks happy!" Andrea said. It did, on its elevation above the canyon floor. The guys hadn't turned off the wagon wheel light fixture that Dad crafted years ago, with neon tubes along each spoke, and light spilled through the windows onto the dark lawn, shining out: "Welcome Home!"

"I weally need to go potty!" Shanan whined.

"Debbie, as soon as we stop, get her onto her potty

chair. Put it next to the car," Mama ordered. She carried Holly into the house in the bassinet, and Brenda rolled the heavy oxygen tank up the terrace. Andrea ran to the swing. I plunked the potty chair on the ground, but Shanan protested.

"Too dark! Inna house, inna house! I gotta *go*!"

I dragged the chair into the house, Shanan hopping like a Mexican jumping bean. She sat down on the potty and peed. A lot of pee.

"Yay! Good job! Everybody clap for Shanan!" I applauded heartily—thanks to her self-control, I wouldn't have to mop the floor again. Then I dug through boxes, looking for diapers, pins, and plastic pants for her "night diaper," and blanket sleepers for the chilly Clementsville night.

It was 9:27 p.m.

"I'm *so* hungry, Mama," Andrea said. Mama didn't hear, in her bedroom changing Holly.

"Shut up, Andi. We're all hungry!" I griped. "Brenda, where are Shanan's diapers?"

"Don't call me Andi!" Andrea threw a punch, which I dodged.

When Shanan realized that her potty party was over, she stood in the middle of the kitchen floor, naked as a jaybird, and stomped her tiny bare foot.

"I hungry!" she shrieked. "An' I want my *house*!"

"Come to big sister." Brenda reached out to pick Shanan up, but the two-year-old tyrant hollered, "I sick of sisters! I want my *Mama*!"

We went on a flower hike to gather the farm's wildflowers every Memorial Day. This photo was taken in front of the knotty pine walls of our farmhouse living room. From left to right: (Back) Ellen, Margie, and Nelda Furniss; (Front) me, Andrea, and Marilyn Furniss in about 1964.

Flowers For Those Who Went Before

Shanan spread-eagled in a full-blown tantrum, heels pounding the kitchen floor. In the bedroom, Holly cried at her full, pitiful capacity. Andrea and I yelled at each other as we searched for diapers amid pots, books, pans, dishes, clothes, towels, canned food, and assorted stuff overflowing the counter, table, and scattered boxes.

"What do we have to eat, Mama?" Brenda asked.

"I don't know—there was some vegetable soup left over yesterday," Mama said between murmurs to Holly. Completely focused, Mama measured formula into a bottle.

"Shanan kicked over her potty chair!" Andrea shouted. Pee trickled across the floor.

"I-G-N-O-R-E," Mama spelled. That was her answer to all our outbursts. It worked nearly every time.

We ignored the spilled pee. Brenda rummaged in the fridge, dumped leftover soup into the first pot she found—it was way too big—and added two cans of corn and a couple of chicken bouillon cubes. Andrea found saltine crackers, and I rustled up bowls and spoons. Brenda fed Holly. Mama fed Shanan some soup, then took her into hers and Dad's bed—the only bed the guys had put together. Upstairs, pieces of our beds littered the girls' and boys' rooms. We would find bedding and sleep on mattresses on the floor.

Andrea and I sat on the front steps, our favorite place to eat at the farm, under the porch's bare lightbulb. Birds murmured sleepily in the aspens, and through the window, we could hear Mama singing to Shanan. A breeze caressed the quaking aspen leaves, and they trembled in reply.

"Debbie, Jocelyn wanted to give me one of her kitties, but Daddy wouldn't let me have it. Why can't we have kitties at the farm?"

"Same reason we can't have chickens or rabbits. Hawks catch them and eat them." Her eyes got big. "I remember a hawk flapping its wings, pinching a half-grown chicken. But be glad you don't have to gather eggs like Rex and I did. The hens never laid them in the same place twice."

"It's so quiet! Why didn't we bring the TV?" she asked.

"The re- re-, the waves, or whatever ... the *reception* up here is bad."

"There's no phone! I can't call Jocelyn."

"No. And Mama can't call the doctor about Holly."

"Brenda can't call her D.J." We laughed. Andrea yawned, and we reentered the bright kitchen.

Mama set the mop against the wall and stroked Andrea's curls. "Honey, you're tired, give me a kiss." They kissed and hugged. I picked my way over the wet floor to put our bowls in the sink.

"Debbie Day-O, come here." Mama motioned me to the front porch and lifted the lid of the freezer. "You did a bang-up job cleaning up that mess!" She gestured at the bare white walls of the freezer, empty except for a few packages of hamburger and frozen vegetables brought from Teton. "It smells so clean! Thank you, honey. Thanks for mopping; you worked hard!" She squeezed me tight and planted a kiss on the top of my head. I breathed in her odor—baby powder, formula, sweat, and soup. Security. She didn't loosen her hug until I stirred.

"You're frazzled. Go to bed," she laughed.

***

Monday, May 30, 1967

CLEMENTSVILLE

Mama pushed us to get enough flowers for our families' graves for days before Memorial Day. She sent us on a "flower hike" up the canyon for wildflowers; we cut blooms from the French lilac bush and picked apple blossoms from the Teton house orchard. We'd inherited Mama's love of flowers and this holiday.

It all culminated when we loaded the flowers and food in the trunk and squeezed ourselves and Holly's oxygen tank into the seats of the Fairlane. Brenda drove us thirty miles east to the Bates Cemetery.

Judy and Silver were there, showing Timmy to Marilyn's family and other Furniss relatives. We decorated the family graves: Mama's Daddy, Will, who we never knew because he died in 1939; her Mama, Grandma Rhodie, who died in January of 1964; our Uncle Irvin Bates, who had married Dad's sister, Ruth, and died on Okinawa in World War II; Mama's four brothers and two sisters who died as babies, and our cousin Ilene "Cookie" Furniss, who died at seven months. Marilyn, Andrea, and I made bouquets of tiny flowers, and Shanan put them on the graves of the babies.

The softball game in Marilyn's family's pasture didn't last long enough, then it was time for fried chicken, Aunt Lola's potato salad, and chocolate cake. After we ate, instead of visiting like usual, Mama rushed us to the car.

"Mama! Can't we stay longer? I want to play with the cousins!" I protested.

"No, honey, Holly needs to go home. She's overstimulated."

"Let me go with Brenda to Uncle Verl's!"

"No. Brenda wants to spend her seventeenth birthday with them, and I'm letting her. You can ride with Judy and Silver to the farm."

I made a face but knew better than to argue. I got into Silver and Judy's back seat and played "Patty-cake" and "This Little Piggy" with Michael—all the way home.

Mama asked me to fix a bottle for Holly. When I brought it to Mama's bedroom, Shanan was putting her doll next to Holly to "play with."

"No, Shannie, you mustn't." Mama was much firmer than she used to be with Shanan. "Holly's tired. Take your dolly and go play with Andrea." Shanan pouted, but obeyed.

Judy laid Timmy down near Holly to change him, and a funny look crossed her face.

"Oh, Mama. She's so tiny." Timmy weighed eight pounds and nine ounces at birth, and at two weeks old, was gaining on Judy's rich milk. Holly had lost a pound. There was a big difference between the babies.

"Holly is tiny, but she's gaining weight. We're working on it." Mama eased Holly out of her cute rosebud dress and into a soft nightgown.

"She works so hard to breathe." Judy sounded like she was wearing her white nurse shoes. "Her limbs are stiff."

Seeing Holly next to Timmy was an eyeopener. She looked sick, her little face pinched and worried. *Does Mama ever think of taking her back to the hospital to see if they can help?* I wondered.

As if reading my mind, Judy said, "Maybe they could help her at Bannock Memorial in Pocatello."

I snapped this photo of Jersey cattle on a walk in Nampa, Idaho, because they reminded me of Swiss Miss, who was a Brown Swiss. Miss was patient with my attempts at milking, and I would have loved her more if she had stayed home instead of venturing forth to visit neighboring bovines.

Milking For All It's Worth

Mama sat on the bed next to Judy. "I know. *She's very sick.* But no doctor or hospital has the answer." Mama waved for me to get toilet paper as her tears fell. "It's a battle. Her little heart has to work so hard. But she has already beaten the odds the doctors gave us!"

"I could help more. I could bring the boys and stay here." Judy's tears flowed. I handed her the toilet paper.

"Judy, no. You have so much to do, helping Silver and your little ones. You mustn't carry the weight of the world on your shoulders—or the weight of this family. You do too much for us. Remember how you spent your first hundred dollars of nurse's wages?"

Judy smiled through her tears. "School clothes for the kids."

"You're helping. Look at how often you've tended Shanan. Don't worry about us. Keep on doing what you're doing—nursing this sweet guy." She brushed a finger across Timmy's round cheek. "Born the day before Grandma Rhodie's birthday—he's perfect."

***

Thursday, June 1, 1967

CLEMENTSVILLE

"Wish I could go to bug camp, and you could stay here and milk Swiss Miss," I groused at breakfast. I'd escaped pig duty only to be tasked with milking the cow.

"No!" Rex said. "You can't spray a bug tree. Sometimes I wish I didn't have to."

"Can't be that hard! Bet I could."

"Bet you couldn't! You can't lift a goop can. And forget about pumping a grunt pump or spraying with the wand—that takes muscle! Boy, the diesel drips on you! If it weren't for the dough, I'd trade you places in a heartbeat."

"I don't want to milk! I tried it, and it's hard."

Mama was warming Holly's bottle under running water. "Debbie, everyone should learn to milk, and without a pig this year, you need to exercise your arms carrying the milk bucket. Rex, why don't you pay her to milk since you're earning so much? If she wasn't milking, you'd have to stay here and milk instead of bugging. Why don't you pay her two dollars per milking?"

Rex pondered. He earned about thirty dollars a day, so four dollars didn't sound bad.

"Okay, but only because I'm kind and generous," he said, snatching my bacon and running out the door.

I grinned. I'd be rich before starting seventh grade.

"Mama! Holly won't take her bottle," Brenda called from the living room. Mama sank onto the couch, offering the bottle, but Holly turned her head. Five minutes, ten minutes, and still Mama battled to get the slightly stinky formula into her baby. Tears coursed down Mama's face.

Andrea watched. "Mama, if you're sad, Holly feels it, and she doesn't eat. Sing her happy songs."

Mama looked surprised. "Okay, honey, like what?"

"Primary songs." Andrea sang, "I Am a Child of God," and Shanan and I joined her.

From then on, we sang during Holly's feedings: all kinds of songs, even "Hello, Holly" to the tune of the Broadway hit "Hello, Dolly." Later Mama wrote, "What a wonderful discovery this was because it was a way for the little ones to enjoy the baby who was too fragile to be held and loved by them. We worked, praying sincerely with Holly. Her heart was large, almost filling her chest. She needed oxygen to keep breathing. Yet still, she struggled sometimes, to smile!"

Dad and Mama hadn't told us that the doctors at Primary Children's said Holly would probably not live past two months. She passed that milestone on June 6. Mama later said that Holly's third month was her happiest.

***

Friday, June 2, 1967

CLEMENTSVILLE

"Debbie, honey, wake up!" Mama shook me. "Miss is mooing. Go do the milking!" I burrowed under the covers and mumbled, "I'm sleepy. Shanan made us keep the light on because she thinks Wee Willie Winkie and the Polka Dots are hiding in the closet."

Mama chuckled and pulled the blankets off me. "Get up!"

Rex is off to earn our fortunes in the forests, and now it's up to me to milk. Man, that sun is bright! I dragged myself out of bed.

Swiss Miss didn't fight as I put her into her stanchion, looped her tail out of the way, and settled the stool next to her. It was late morning, her udder was bursting, and she wanted to be milked. I squeezed milk out for what seemed like forever. Then I rested.

The one-legged milking stool was not built for comfort and sitting on it was a balancing act. I squeezed and squeezed some more. I rested. *Rex didn't take this long milking last night!* I squeezed for a few more minutes. Miss shifted nervously, pulling her tail out of the loop and brushing my face.

"Stupid cow!" I muttered. "This is taking forever! My hands are killing me!"

I had no idea if I had milked long enough when I finally "stripped the cream." Rex said that was important, to slide Miss's teats, one by one, several times between the sides of my index finger and thumbs, to bring down the cream. Miss and I were both relieved when I opened the stanchion, and she bolted out the door.

I picked up the heavy pail and walked back to the house. *My arm bones will straighten out and stretch six inches at this rate.*

Andrea peered into the bucket. "That's not as much as Rexie gets!"

"Shut up."

Diary, Saturday, June 3, 1967: Milked cow. Morning—easy; night—problem. Holly is eating better. Daddy, Kerry, Rex, and Bruce came home.

Diary, Monday, June 5, 1967: Went to town & got Brenda [after her bus ride from Blackfoot.] Got more milk than I have yet. Holly was going to doctor but didn't. She was kind of cranky.

Diary, Tuesday, June 6, 1967: Mom took Holly to doctor. She weighs 6 lb. 2 oz. She felt rough after that.

Mama holding Shanan, who wore Dad's felt cowboy hat, at the farm in 1965.

Rockin' and Rollin' At The Farm

Friday, June 9, 1967

CLEMENTSVILLE

Andrea busted in, yelling, "I see dust! A blue car—Aunt Lola!" We poured out of the house and down the terrace to greet them, and we poured back in with cousins and aunt in tow.

Mama asked Aunt Lola if she'd like to hold Holly.

"She's so tiny." Aunt Lola's brow creased.

"She had a good day yesterday. She gained an ounce."

Aunt Lola started to say something but snuggled the baby tighter instead.

"You're going to the reunion in Rupert?" Mama asked.

"Yes. The Allen cousins will give everyone rides in

their motorboats!"

Mama looked wistful—she loved visiting her brothers, cousins, and Furniss relatives. She would've moved heaven and earth to attend this family reunion any other year.

Holly fussed, arching her back, and Mama spread a rubber sheet. "I'll give her an enema. She has to have two or three every day; it seems like she can't push it out." Two months before, Mama would not have done this in front of anyone outside our family circle, but now, Holly's needs came before anything or anyone.

Mama murmured sweet encouragement and used petroleum jelly and an ear syringe to help the baby do the work she couldn't do on her own. *Mama's so fierce when we disobey or back-talk, but she's wondrously gentle with Holly.*

Marilyn and I put our heads together in the corner, then Marilyn whispered to her mom.

Aunt Lola nodded. "Joyce, we'd love to take Debbie with us."

"Please let me go, Mama!" I begged. "Brenda can milk Swiss Miss and earn money. It's Marilyn's birthday, and if I go, that's her present!"

This summer, most of our fun would be provided by relatives who took us to events. Mama sighed. She believed that kids should have fun and work, but it was a balancing act with each child—how much work to make them do, how much fun to let them have, how to love them each and love them all.

"All right—thanks for taking her, Lola. Get packed, Debbie!" Mama said. I ran to find a paper bag to fill with clothes. Marilyn and I waved goodbye to Andrea and Shanan who were looking sad on the steps.

We spent the night with cousins in Pocatello, then drove to Minidoka Dam in Rupert, where we ate a delicious reunion picnic. We swam and took turns taking fast rides in a motorboat. The long ride home was a three-hour stupor of sunburned exhaustion.

As I staggered into the house, Mama wrapped me in a hug. "Guess what? There's a surprise! Lola, come see!" Mama ushered everyone into the living room. Brenda was feeding Holly, sitting in a new rocking chair with a ruffled cushion.

"Saturday, I laid Holly on my bed so she could soak up sunshine from the window. Shanan was being good, sitting next to her. We heard whooping and hollering, and here came Daddy down the dugway in the grain truck, with Rex and Andrea in the back. And Brenda, in that rocking chair!" Mama was thrilled, and the chair was a blessing. Holly loved being rocked.

Diary, Monday, June 12, 1967: Incessant rain for two weeks. Roads muddy. Went to town with Brenda. Left car at top of dugway to keep from getting stuck again. Holly lots better, she weighs six lb. two oz. Glad to be home.

Idaho Highway 33 was paved, but to get to our farmhouse, we turned off 33 onto a gravel road for a mile and followed a dirt road for more than a mile. Dry weather churned the dirt into fine dust, which forced Mama and Brenda to wear scarves to protect their hair. During this wet June, rain pounded the dust in four low spots into quagmires whose consistency ranged from gritty mayonnaise during a storm to molasses a day later.

A noisy storm had thundered through, and the mud was somewhere in between those extremes when Brenda steered successfully through two bogs on our way home after facing the clerk at the Teton Merc.

We weren't so lucky on the next-to-last mud puddle. Brenda pushed on the gas, fishtailed a bit, slowed, and the wheels slipped. She pressed the gas slowly.

"Dang! Come on, Fairlane. Come on. We can do it," she begged, and we crawled forward.

"We did it! We're almost out!" I yelled. But, as Mama would have said, "Pride goeth before a fall." Just before pulling out of the hole, the back wheels whirred, then sunk, spinning the car's rear end into the mire.

Brenda pounded the wheel and yelled, "This farm is *hell!*"

Brenda swore!

I got over my shock when I remembered what we would have to do next. "With Dad bugging, we'll have to walk a mile and a half to Uncle Henry's and ask him to pull us out, *if* he's home and not out farming, or gone to town for parts, or fishing because it rained."

"Can't do that. Too embarrassing." She rubbed her

forehead. "Have you watched Dad steer through ruts?"

"No, I can't say that I have. Dad drives, and I look out the window if I don't have a book to read."

"He's loose. His arms and shoulders go back and forth, like this." She did a floppy imitation of Dad. "He aims for the shallow parts of the mudhole, his feet work the gas and sometimes the clutch to hit the better spots at the right speed: not so fast that he fishtails, not so slow that the wheels spin and the car sinks. Like it just did."

As a nondriver and a non-watcher of Dad, I had little to contribute. I finally thought of something. "Dad got stuck Sunday, but he rocked the car out of it."

"Oh, yeah—remember last week? In this puddle, I tried to rock it and spun us deeper." Brenda winced, remembering the lecture Dad dished out while he hooked up the tractor.

"What will we do? We better start walking."

Brenda nibbled a fingernail and straightened her shoulders. "We've got to get unstuck. I watched Dad Sunday, and I will rock us out! You push," she ordered.

I got out. *Weeds saved me alongside the Teton River*, I thought. *Maybe they'll help us now.* Before Brenda twisted the key, I yelled, "Stop!"

"What?" She was annoyed.

"I'll pull weeds and cram them under the tires."

She looked dubious but nodded. "Every bit of traction helps."

I whispered a prayer, too. We didn't want to bother

Uncle Henry, and Mama wouldn't want us to if we could help it.

I shoved in a last handful of weeds and stood behind the car. "Go!" I yelled.

Brenda eased the Ford into compound, then into reverse, and repeated it time and again, rocking forward and back, forward and back, crawling a few inches forward every time. When she gained enough momentum, she yelled, "Push!" I pushed, adding my feeble muscle power to the efforts of the engine as mud splattered my shoes and pants.

We stood on the kitchen steps of the farmhouse. From left to right: (Back) Jeanne, me (ducking my head behind Judy), Brenda, Mama, Dad; (Front) Judy, Bruce (home on leave, holding Shanan and Michael), Rex, and Andrea. Silver took this photo in 1965.

Pink Paint and Modesty

Brenda steered out of the mire and stopped on the other side, jubilant. "We did it!"

"Good job! You drove way better than last week."

To bypass the fourth mud hole, Brenda took a different route to the top of the dugway, parked, and turned the engine off. "I'm not driving down that dugway; it's slick as snot! I can't believe we got unstuck."

I handed her a box of groceries from the back seat.

She smiled. "Great teamwork—me rocking the car, you with your weeds and pushing! We did all right." She looked at the mud-encrusted sides of the car—the newest car our family had ever had, bought with the proceeds from selling the farmland.

"Brenda, you were crazy back there. You said the farm is hell." I was shocked.

"This place *is hell* when the car gets stuck! It's *hell* when the horse flies and deer flies bite. It's *hell* when it's hot, when there's no breeze in the canyon, and we're dragging around like half-baked potatoes. If it's not dust so thick it could choke a horse, that dirties up your hair and clothes, it's mud that gets your car stuck. Remember the flash flood? That storm felt like *hellfire and brimstone*!" Balancing the groceries, she slammed the car door with her foot.

She had me. When I was six, a hailstorm triggered a flash flood down the canyon, turning Timothy Creek into a raging torrent that ripped our road out. Brenda and Rex frolicked in the muddy current, excited to see a river magically appear. When I followed, the water swept me off my feet and tumbled me downstream, gulping muddy water and struggling to touch bottom. Mama ran along the stream, her face white as paper, yelling, "Grab weeds!" which I did, hanging on for dear life. Mama helped me climb up a new bank.

The current ripped out our road down the canyon bottom from the house to the gate.

Isaac had a ram; I've got weeds. But I can't admit that this farm is as bad as Brenda says.

"You just like saying *Hell!* You're lucky Mama can't hear you."

"Mama's too busy to worry about me cussing," Brenda muttered, picking her way to the top of the muddy dugway.

She softened and whispered, "Smell those heavenly roses!" June's first dark pink wild roses perfumed the moist air. She set down her box, picked a handful of flowers, then yelled, "Race you down!"

We pounded down the dugway grade, laughing and pushing ahead of each other, feeling the muddy but solid earth of *our farm* thump up through our feet and legs.

The sun lit up diamonds on aspen leaves, and the scent of roses and rain filled the air. Birdsongs rang out.

Brenda twirled like Julie Andrews in the Swiss Alps.

"This place is heaven, Debbie, and I'm never going to say it's hell again! Let's climb back up for the groceries."

Diary, Wednesday, June 14, 1967: Looked for cow, found her at Ricks's farm. Milked late. Painted kitchen pink until 1:20 a.m. when Brenda & I finally went to bed. Holly felt better.

Diary, Thursday, June 15, 1967: Painted and painted and painted kitchen perky pink. Milked. Painted more, got to bed about 12:30. Holly took it all well, considering.

Ellen stayed with us quite a bit that summer. Kerry was bugging in the mountains with Bruce and Rex, and the tiny house in Rexburg felt empty to her. Ellen was fun and brought interesting library books, like *To Kill a Mockingbird*, to read out loud. Ever our diligent wardrobe sheriff, she instructed us if bra straps showed, if skirts were too short, or if nylons had runs. So Brenda and I were shocked when we saw it: Ellen was painting in her slip.

"Hey, Ellen, you call that modest?" Brenda asked.

"No, I don't. But the guys are in the mountains, and we're miles from anyone, and it's 9:30 p.m. Why not?"

"When I paint, I put on old clothes," I said righteously.

"I only own a couple of maternity dresses, one pair of pants, and my orange smock. Kerry says I look like I'm hiding a basketball under it! This slip is the only thing I fit into that can't be hurt by paint. You missed a spot, Debbie. Paint your strokes the same direction. Too bad we have to do two coats."

"How was the road coming in?" Brenda asked.

"Terrible! I was lucky to get through the mud bogs."

"Yeah, it's a wet summer."

Ellen reflected. "Well, it was pretty wet the year Andrea was a baby, back in 1960. Of course, you've never experienced a winter here, with snowdrifts ten feet deep, like we older kids have."

Brenda and I looked at each other. The younger half of the family would never have experiences to equal those of the older kids—at least according to *them*.

Mama came in to fix a bottle and looked at our work. "I'm tickled pink! Thank you, thank you, girls. Tomorrow we'll get wallpaper up, and we'll be ready when company comes."

We were working under a tight deadline, as always with Mama's projects. So many people were coming to visit Holly that Mama had decided to get rid of the dingy white wallpaper festooned with ivy and replace it with paint, and pink-on-white floral wallpaper, before the weekend. It lifted our spirits, especially Mama's.

This is the only photo of Wayne, Joyce, and all ten of their children. From left to right: (Back) Judy holding Timothy, Wayne, Bruce, Joyce holding Holly, Rex, Ellen, Kerry, Debbie, Alan, and Jeanne; (Front) Shanan, Brenda, Michael, and Andrea. Silver Hidalgo took the photo at the Nelson Midsummer Reunion in June 1967. It is unfortunate that he isn't in this photo, as well as in many other photos that he took of our family.

Midsummer Reunion

Our grandfather, Joe Nelson, nurtured a Swedish tradition among his siblings and children: every year on the Saturday closest to the summer solstice, the Nelson family hosted a reunion at a park in Rexburg. "Midsummer" was the biggest event of my summer.

When Brenda yelled that a car was coming, Ellen rushed to put on her orange smock and maternity pants. It was Dad's cousin, Clarence Nelson, and his family from Moses Lake, Washington. Brenda and I took our second cousin, who had the same name as me—Debbie Nelson—on a hike to our "pioneer relic," the Hugh Davis cabin site at the upper end of our canyon. Then we picked up cousins Lila and Carmen Nelson, drove to Rexburg, and "dragged Main."

Dad took Clarence, his son Darwin, and Rex, fishing on the Teton River, where hellgrammites were hatching into trout flies: the perfect bait for rainbow trout. Mama, Cousin Margaret, and Ellen tended Holly and the little girls, and finished wallpapering. Jeanne helped after she and Alan arrived.

***

Saturday, June 17, 1967

CLEMENTSVILLE

"Hurry up! They'll eat before we get there!" Rex hammered on the girls' room door. We were putting on our Midsummer outfits—our nicest casual clothes.

"Rex! Get down here!" Dad yelled.

I finished rolling my last hair curler and pounded down the stairs after Rex. "Dad, can I play softball this year? I've got my mitt."

"You've got a mitt, but you sure can't use it!" Rex jeered.

"That's enough, son. Grab that pan of rolls and some butter and jam, and load it in the trunk while I pack the fish. Yes, Deb, load the baseball gear."

Dad had fried a mess of trout while Mama bathed Holly and dressed her in her cutest pink dress. Usually

Mama made huckleberry pies, potato salad and fried chicken, but this year was different—we only took two pans of dinner rolls that Brenda had baked, and fried trout.

"Get this show on the road—we've got to drive twenty-seven miles before the fish get cold!" Dad yelled.

"Rex, please roll Holly's oxygen tank out," Mama said. "Debbie Day-O, make sure Andrea and Shannie have clean faces and hands. Grab a brush and barrettes for their hair. Brenda, get the formula and bottles into the diaper bag."

Some of us settled in the Fairlane, while others rode with Clarence's family and Jeanne.

"Move over, Rex, give me a window seat," I said. When we got to the highway and Dad cranked it up to fifty-five miles an hour, I stuck my head out the car window to dry my hair

"You look like Patches!" Andrea squealed. I jerked the curlers out when Dad pulled up at the park.

Rex breathed a sigh of relief—they'd waited! A swarm of Dad's brothers and brothers-in-law surrounded him, shaking his hand, and helping him maneuver the oxygen tank. A swarm of sisters-in-law surrounded Mama, hugging her. Aunt Clara said the Nelsons hadn't been huggers until Mama converted them. Mama introduced Holly to our extended family, saying it was time they got to know our very different, but very Nelson, Holly-girl.

At one perfect moment, the hugging paused; someone

welcomed everyone to Midsummer, and someone else said a blessing on the food. We ate until we were stuffed. When Uncle Henry's family produced three freezers of homemade ice cream, we ate some more, dishing it into cones and piling it on top of cake, pie, and cookies.

My cousins and I pumped in the swings and made hundreds of trips down the tall, rickety slippery slide. Dad gave us change, and we took Andrea and Shanan for rides on the magical merry-go-round, with its hand-carved horses and calliope music. On Brenda's third trip back, I figured out that she was flirting with the cute guy who ran the carousel and sold concessions—his name was Shae.

I muffed catches and struck out in the "singles versus marrieds" softball game—it was lot more fun with my family than at school. Dad hit a triple, and I even hit a single.

Silver took the only family picture that included all ten of us children.

We slept under the stars in the farmhouse backyard. From left to right: Rex, Darwin Nelson (a second cousin, behind Rex's arm), me, Andrea, and Debbie Nelson (Darwin's sister). Patches' back is in the foreground.

Starlight Melody

"Let's go home." Mama patted Holly anxiously. "Brenda, round up our serving dishes. Debbie, get the softball gear, and Rex, load the oxygen tank."

"Mama, can Debbie and Darwin stay at our house for a couple of days? Clarence and Margaret are staying at Uncle Lester's," Rex said.

Mama's forehead furrowed as Holly cried, arching her back. "Holly needs to get home."

"Pleeeease?"

Mama sighed and smiled. "Okay. They've come so far, who knows when you'll be together again? Now load the oxygen tank!"

I threw bats and mitts into a canvas bag, thinking, *Marilyn will always be my best friend, but Debbie is fun, too.*

In the car, Andrea asked, "May we sleep out?"

"Sure. There isn't room in the house, with the married kids here," Mama said.

Diary, Saturday, June 17, 1967: Holly not well. Saddening. Debbie and Darwin Nelson stayed with us.

Diary, Monday, June 19, 1967: Everyone mad this morning cause we (Brenda, Debbie, and me) got home late. Holly is the same. Today we went to town, shopped and ate, and dropped Darwin and Debbie off.

***

Sunday, June 25, 1967

CLEMENTSVILLE

It was 9:00 p.m., and Ellen was filling the wringer washer.

"I hate these stinky clothes!" I griped.

"Tough bounce! The pesticide in the goop kills the beetles, so it stinks worse than plain diesel. Dump in a cup and a half of detergent, and be glad you don't have to wear those clothes. Be glad you don't have to spray trees, getting your skin soaked in so much diesel that you smell that way even after a bath." Ellen put her hand on the small of her back. "Be glad you're not me—today's my due date."

We washed goopy clothes in the wringer washer and rinsed them through two rinses in twin rinse tubs, pushing each piece through the wringer every time. We refilled the rinse tubs with clean water and repeated the process, shoving the clothes through the whining wringer one last time. Mama made Ellen go to bed before we finished.

It was well after eleven when I took the first load to the clothesline. I flapped the wrinkles out of each piece and pinned them with clothespins. Millions of stars swung close to the farm—there was the Big Dipper, upside down in the sky. There was the Little Dipper, usually so hard to find!

It's odd that we aren't scared of the dark. Why? Patches brushed his nose against my bare leg, and I didn't jump, knowing it was him. Patches was a good watch dog, and Dad was adamant that bears didn't roam here. Kids in my class, including Bea, feared the dark in Teton, with its lights, houses, people, and dogs. *They're sissy.* The electric light glared against my pupils when I went in the house for the second basket of clothes, and I was glad to return to the darkness.

A bird cried out sleepily. Holly fussed near Mama's open bedroom window. A minute later, through the living room window, the rocking chair creaked as Mama sank into it; then came her lullaby: "There, oh there, oh there, oh there." Holly hushed.

Jeanne said that like somebody in the Bible, Mama

"slumbereth not nor sleepeth." Mama wasn't sleeping that midnight.

I pinned the last shirt, praying that rain wouldn't blow in, that everything would dry, and that the guys could take these clothes to bug camp the next day. It felt good to crawl into bed!

***

Friday, June 30, 1967

CLEMENTSVILLE

On the last day of June, Holly weighed six pounds and twelve ounces. She had regained her birth weight but had a bad cold. That evening, Mama rocked Holly. She said she ought to make supper, but Holly was fussy.

"Mama, I've got six sisters, like in the princess story Brenda read me," Andrea said. "How many sisters do you have?"

Mama sighed. "I had two sisters—Maude and Rula."

"I don't remember those aunts."

"No. Maude lived only one day, and that was before I was born. When I was four years old, your Grandma Rhodie gave birth to twins—a brother, Alma Roe, and a sister, Rula. They were born two months too early. Rula lived for a few hours. Now, honey, take Shanan and play outside."

Mama always answered our questions, but it wasn't always easy for her.

Andrea took Shanan by the hand. "C'mon. Play in the sandbox while I swing."

After they left, Brenda whispered. "Tell us the rest, Mama."

Mama rocked, the movement taking her memories back to 1924. "My Daddy nailed together a tiny casket. He had me go behind the curtain that separated our bedrooms so I wouldn't see when he laid Rula in it. He carried it out into the November snow, and he and my brothers dug Rula's grave and buried her.

"Mama expressed breast milk, dipped a cloth in it and touched Alma's lips to encourage his sucking reflex. Mama, Daddy, and the midwife took turns around the clock, keeping the tiny baby in the warmth next to the open oven door of the wood stove. After six days, Daddy built a casket for Alma. I took Verl, who was two, by the hand. I told him, 'I won't let you die! I won't let you die!'"

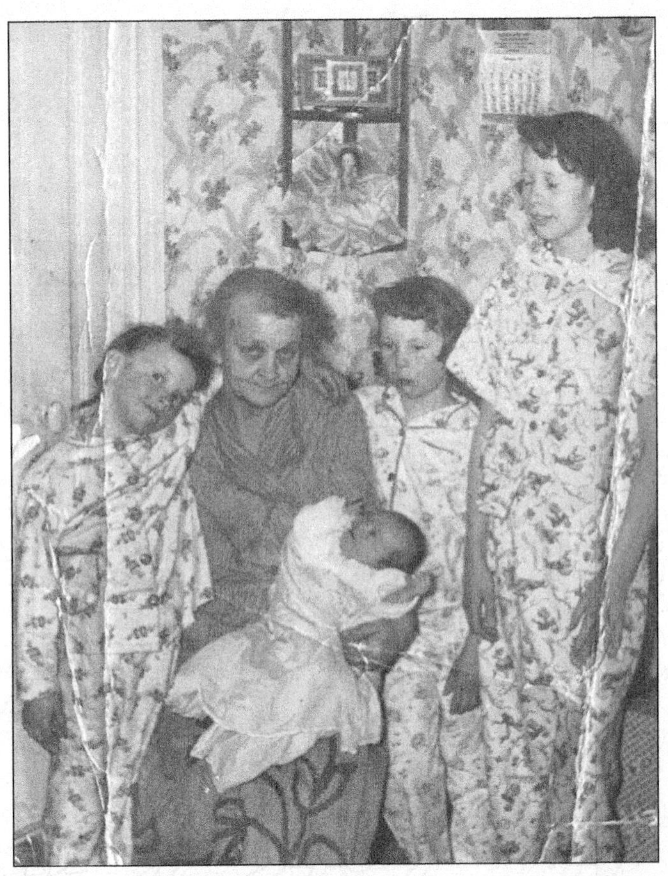

Having an overnight party with Rhoda Furniss—our "Grammy" or "Grandma Rhodie"—meant snuggles, good cooking, and fun. She came for several overnights in a row when we had a new baby. In this photo, she's holding baby Brenda with Jeanne (left side), Ellen, and Judy (right side). They are wearing new pajamas that she gave them in 1950.

Quail In July

Mama's voice was low. "My Mama and Daddy buried three other baby sons and Maude. Some lived for hours, some for days, and two boys for three weeks each. All were born premature because of Mama's gestational diabetes."

Brenda sniffed, and Mama looked around, thinking about the impact of the sad story she was sharing. "But seven of their babies—my six brothers and me—were full-term pregnancies! Look how healthy we are! Together, we've given Grammy thirty-seven children!"

She eased Holly into the bassinet. "It wasn't just babies—your Grandma Rhodie nursed sick lambs, calves, puppies, and kittens by the wood-burning stove. Anything living—she and my Daddy fought and prayed to keep it alive!"

Brenda blew her nose. "Oh, Mama. When you had

a baby, the best part was that Grammy came! When she washed the sheets, and it was time for bed, she'd let us lay there while she made the bed over us! I wish she hadn't died!"

"I thought they named graham crackers after her, because she was sweet and good like they are," I sniffed.

Andrea and Shanan ran in, laughing.

"Mama, we're hungry! Do we have graham crackers?" Andrea asked.

Brenda saw that Mama was weeping, and said, "No. But help me, and we'll make pancakes for supper. Here, Shanan, stand on this chair."

***

Saturday, July 1, 1967

CLEMENTSVILLE

"Mama, the dang cow is gone again!"

"You milked her this morning. She couldn't have gone far."

"Oh, she can go far! She's proved that. Dad and Rex need to re-string the barbed wire fence in the upper pasture!" One of the problems with living at the farm while Dad worked far away was that he had no time to fix things like fences.

"Swiss Miss knows one of the neighbors has a bull. She just can't remember which one." Brenda giggled at her cleverness.

"You'd better go find her," Mama said.

Muttering under my breath about stupid cows, I started for the Ricks farm. I was almost to the gate when Dad pulled up, home from bug camp. I spilled my miserable tale.

"I'll pull over and help you look for Miss in the aspen thickets."

"Thanks, Dad. Now, maybe, I won't strangle that dang cow when we find her!"

We walked into the trees. A covey of quail scurried in and out of chokecherry bushes. Dad signaled me to be still as the hen chuckled softly, gathering her chicks—tiny feather-puffs—under her wings.

"They'll smother, it's so hot!" I whispered.

"Not at all. They're in the safest possible place—close to her heart. If they get too warm, she'll fan them with her wings. If they get cold tonight, they'll snuggle in tight."

"Do some of 'em die?"

He was quiet. "Not under their mama's wings, they don't. But quite a lot do die—hawks, weasels, coyotes, foxes, skunks, even cats prey on quail. I'm relieved to see this hen with lots of babies—means there's been plenty of food."

I wished I could hold one—baby chicks were fuzzy

and fun, but baby quail were even tinier with a quieter, sweeter "peep-peep." But their mama sheltered them under her wings, deep in the brush, and if I stuck my hand in there, her sharp beak would convince me not to mess with her babies, double-quick.

Bruce roared by in his car, alone, in a cloud of dust.

"What do you want to bet he is hurrying to get a bath and supper before heading to a dance? And what do you want to bet that they found the cow, and Rex is driving her home?"

Dad was always right, so I didn't take his bets. We drove home, and I grabbed the milk bucket, and headed out to meet Rex and Miss. *Maybe Rex will cheap out on me and milk to save himself two dollars. Or I'll milk. Either way, Miss will be turned out for another day of eating grass in our pasture—at least, I pray it will be our pasture, and not Ricks's.*

Diary, Tuesday, July 4, 1967: Yay, America! Forward U.S! Independence Day! Had fireworks. We kids started for Rexburg late. Had fun picnic in Smith Park. No news from Ellen. Went to a very good rodeo.

All day, Brenda, Rex, Andrea, Shanan, and I celebrated independence from work and worry with firecrackers, cap guns, and rolls of caps that Dad bought for us. Rex exploded cow pies in at least fifty different ways.

In late afternoon, Brenda asked Mama, who was pushing diapers through the wringer, if we could go to the rodeo in St. Anthony. Mama swiped a soapy hand across her brow.

"Kids ought to have fun on a holiday, and you can check on Ellen." She smiled. "Finish washing these diapers, and hang them, then you can go. Two rinses, mind you, to prevent diaper rash."

We whooped all the way to Rexburg's Smith Park, where we ate sandwiches and cookies and climbed on the antique steam engine that was more fun (and ten times more dangerous) than the swings.

Ellen looked the same: bulging, but no baby.

"The rodeo in St. Anthony starts at eight. You guys want to go?" Brenda asked.

"No. Ellen is ten days overdue and doesn't feel like sitting on those benches," Kerry replied. "Besides, there are no softballs at a rodeo. A sport that doesn't involve a ball—especially a softball—isn't a sport."

"We probably better not," Ellen said. "Shanan looks tired—why don't you leave her with us?"

"Sure!" Brenda said. There'd be handsome cowboys at the rodeo. Angells were providing the stock—and it would be easier to flirt without a two-year-old in tow.

***

At the fairgrounds, the mayor of St. Anthony introduced the rodeo clown. The clown said, "Do you know the difference between me and a politician?" The mayor shook his head.

"Instead of being neck-deep in it, I try to avoid the bull!" The crowd howled, and he warmed up. "I hope Angells have better stock than they did at the Driggs rodeo—the bulls were so sleepy, they were BULLDOZERS!"

"This is better than Bruce's high school rodeos!" I yelled over the noisy crowd.

"Yeah, remember how he rode broncs with a square of foam pad jammed between his britches and his undershorts?" Rex said.

Andrea begged for a snow cone, and Brenda took her to the concession stand. They took forever—I hoped that meant Brenda was buying me a cone. Finally, I walked over to find out.

Brenda was flirting with the guy grinding ice—that guy we'd seen at the merry-go-round, Shae. Brenda was gesturing, telling a story, when that Angell kid walked up, swept off his cowboy hat, and said hello. Before Brenda could answer, Andrea fumbled her half-eaten raspberry snow cone into the dirt. Shae took Brenda's attention from the Angell guy by gallantly offering Andrea a free snow cone.

Andrea has all the luck, I thought as I walked up. Brenda introduced me.

Shae said, “Wow, Debbie is your exact duplicate!”

We laughed. Brenda was six feet tall with dark brown hair and blue eyes. I was five foot seven with light brown hair and green eyes, yet lots of people said we looked alike.

It was 11:00 p.m. before the last bull bucked off the last rider, and we got in the car.

“Shae’s kind of cute,” I said.

“He’s too short,” Brenda said.

“That leaves your ‘angel.’”

“He’s short, too. But it was a great rodeo!”

Kerry sleepily dumped Shanan into my arms and shut the door at 11:23 p.m. He didn’t know it, but Ellen was in the early stages of labor.

***

July 5–9, 1967

CLEMENTSVILLE

Lance Wayne Frazier was born at 11:30 a.m. on July 5, weighing eight pounds twelve ounces, healthy and strong. Brenda went to Rexburg to help for a few days, and as soon as Ellen felt strong enough, they came to the farm.

Mama looked worried as she leaned over Ellen in the rocking chair.

"Honey, is that working?"

"He's had trouble nursing ever since he was born." Ellen tried to get Lance to latch on while placing a rubber bottle nipple over her own. "The nurse said this should help." Lance arched and rooted.

"Oh, honey," Mama sighed.

"The nurse's solution seems to make it worse!" Tears slipped down Ellen's face.

"Mama, Holly needs help," Brenda said from Mama's bedroom. Holly was having bad days more often, struggling to breathe and uncomfortable with colic.

Once again, Mama couldn't help with a precious newborn grandchild.

***

Wednesday, July 12, 1967

CLEMENTSVILLE

I slept in and milked late. Swiss Miss nervously kicked the bucket over and put her foot in it, ruining the milk. Mama wasn't happy about that, and she curtly reminded me to mop floors and do dishes.

Shanan whined, and Mama spelled, "I-G-N-O-R-E." Shanan's neediness increased daily.

Holly was fussy, and when I asked Mama for the sixth time if anyone was going to Rexburg, she snapped at me. So I vented.

"Nobody matters to you but Holly!"

Mama ignored me.

"I'm sure you haven't noticed that I haven't held or fed Holly for a couple of days. I play with Shanan and pretend that *she's* our baby."

Shanan whined, "Mama, I so hungry!"

Mama asked, "Debbie-Day-o, would you heat up some ham and beans for us?"

"No, I would not. Nobody seems to notice that I do everything."

"Please?"

"Mama, my glasses have been broken for a week. Nobody cares. People make trips to town, and I'm stuck here tending kids, changing diapers, making meals, hanging clothes, trying to see out of my crappy glasses held together with masking tape!"

Mama should have said something about "crappy"—it was a bad word. But she ignored me, and worked with Holly, telling Brenda, "She's gained weight." Even though Mama usually acted like Holly gaining weight was good news, she didn't seem happy.

"Well, la de da. I gain weight every day, and nobody seems to care," I interrupted.

Mama sighed. If she defended herself, or Holly at all, I would torch my vigilantly tended fuse of jealousy into an inferno.

Brenda loved our swing and was ready to push Ruth Briscoe, a second cousin holding Andrea, and Nelda Furniss, a cousin holding her brother, Gary, in 1960.

Save Us From Those Who Mean Well

I care!" said Brenda. "The more weight you gain, the closer you come to being my 'exact duplicate.'"

She was teasing AND changing the subject, and it infuriated me. I wanted to rant at Mama, force her to sympathize with me. *It'd be nice if Brenda was on my side*! I glared at Brenda. She whispered, "Don't."

Don't. It's that simple? Decide not to give in to anger that boils like lava? Decide not to fight for my rightful place in Mama's attention when I am so picked on? I fought to hang on to my precious fury, but Holly looked limp. Mama was massaging Holly's back gently with two fingers, trying to restore an energy that was ebbing. I realized I'd seen Mama do this many times. *Don't.*

My smoldering temper quenched. There would be

times when I would rant and rage and vent my spleen. But not today.

"Mama, the beans are warm. After we eat, Debbie and I will go to Rexburg for oxygen if it's all right. We'll get her glasses fixed," Brenda said.

Mama smiled, and I ran to change clothes. We were headed to town!

We stopped at the Teton Merc to buy hamburger, flour, yeast, and mesh for the torn screen door.

"Make sure your father brings a payment next time he comes to town. I mailed a bill last week," the clerk said loudly as I walked out.

I slammed the car door. I hated the way she always reminded us that we owed money. I hated the fact that she had to.

"Money's tight, but Dad will get a big check and pay the Merc soon, when bugging ends," Brenda said. "Let's go spend my babysitting money on root beer floats."

We drank root beer, flirted with a cute young guy at the oxygen place, dragged Main, and headed home. That night, I rocked Holly for Mama. I wrote in my diary, *"Holly very sweet & good today. Cow kicked over & put foot in bucket. Went to town. Did lots of dishes & mopped floors."*

The next day I realized I had forgotten to get my glasses fixed.

I missed time with Mama, and she couldn't give me one minute right now. I had to find a way to feel close to her, so I created a reading nook outside, in a small depression under her bedroom window near the clothesline. It was always shady, and I made an old blanket into a "nest." Nobody found me there when dishes needed washed or girls needed tending. If someone came around, I pretended to hang or take down clothes. I could relax in this secret spot, but if Mama needed me, I'd hear her voice through the open window.

***

I wasn't the only one who needed Mama. Our home in Teton, two blocks from Highway 33, was the rest, water, grape juice, cookies, coffee, dinner, "visiting with Joyce and sharing your troubles," stop for every family member and friend from Jackson Hole to Pocatello. Mama ministered to most of her Teton neighbors and turned the other cheek to the rest. She juggled these relationships and took care of Dad and nine children until Holly was born; then, every knock on the door and ring of the telephone pulled her away from life-giving responsibilities.

Mama found refuge at the farm, even though it took her further from grocery stores and doctors' offices. Although she seldom left Holly for long, it nourished her spirit to hear chislers chirp and to breathe herbal air wafting through the windows. She was healed by the solitude: quaking aspen whispering to the moonlight, wildflowers dotting hills and meadows, hawks keening in the blue sky.

To get to Mama at the farm, people had to negotiate dusty or muddy roads, and that discouraged some. Yet as Dad said, *"You can run but you can't hide."* Plenty of folks turned off the highway to bump over ruts for two miles to our house. That summer, Mama was deeply moved when two friends from the Teton Ward of our church parked their car near a deep mudhole and walked the rest of the way to the house to offer love and support that Mama truly needed.

Diary, Friday, July 14, 1967: Holly had a terrible day. Mom thought we might have to take her to doctor. Cow kicked over & put foot in bucket again. Oven gave out. Brenda baked at Uncle Henry's. Lots of company came. [Ten names listed.]

Somebody had loaned Mama the book *Angel Unaware* by Dale Evans Rogers, and Brenda was reading it out loud to us. Dale and her husband, Roy Rogers, were Hollywood stars whose daughter, Robin, was born with health issues.

"Their baby had Down Syndrome, and most of the doctors said to put her in an institution. But one doctor told them to take her home and love her! And that's what we're doing with you," Mama told Holly as she lifted her out of her bath.

Andrea yelled that a car was coming. It was a hot Friday, and I was tired of company. I'd washed dishes and had kept Andrea and Shanan out of Mama's hair, so

I snagged *Angel Unaware* and some clothes to hang on the line and curled up in my "hidey hole."

I didn't get to read, though. Mama would've preferred entertaining in the living room or even the kitchen, but she had to invite company into her bedroom while she took care of Holly, to keep the baby's schedule on track. I didn't recognize this visitor's voice—she might have been a distant cousin or a family friend. Whoever she was, she meant well. She said she had "come to comfort her dear Joyce." Her voice was as clear as if I was in the house.

Holly was fussy, and as Mama diapered her, ever so gently, the woman gasped, "Oh, my!" I understood—frail, naked Holly didn't look like other three-month-old babies. Sensing her friend's discomfort, Mama said, "It's all right; she's all right. We'll get her under the oxygen, and she won't look so blue." I could imagine Mama putting the oxygen tube near Holly's nose and smoothing on baby oil before dressing the baby in my favorite rosebud-print dress.

"Here, would you like to hold her?" Mama asked after a few minutes.

"Oh, Joyce, this is a very sick baby! She's suffering! Can't you see how stiff she is?"

At this, I peeked through the window—all I could see was the visitor's back. Her spine was rigid. The end of the oxygen tube trailed behind her arm, far from Holly's nostrils.

"You don't understand, Joyce. Don't cling to her like

this; don't keep giving oxygen and everything. Let her go. On the farm we know when animals are—are dying. We, we, we let them go! If you keep nurturing her, what kind of life—?"

She handed Holly back to Mama, not seeing the oxygen tube slide to the floor.

This woman is saying Mama should "let Holly go." Take away the rocking, the singing, the enemas, and what else? The formula and oxygen?

Head down, not meeting the eyes that challenged her, Mama said, "Excuse me, it's time to feed her," took Holly in her arms and picked up the oxygen tube.

I sunk down onto the blanket, sick at heart.

The woman started to speak, but Mama beat her to it. "How's your son? Has he won any more prizes for selling vacuum cleaners door-to-door?" There was a chill in her voice. I thought of the mama quail and wondered if this was Mama's best effort at pecking someone.

However quickly their visit ended, it wasn't quick enough for me. Or for Mama. She closed the door after the woman and sat on the bed, sobbing for a long time.

The bedroom door opened, and Dad walked in. "I picked up the mail. Look at these bills—the power company for both the farm and Teton houses, Primary Children's, Dr. Melcher!" His voice faded. "What's the matter?"

The bed creaked as he sat.

Mama choked out what the woman had said. "It's like

when that doctor called Holly 'it.' Oh, I hate people who judge and jury their way through life. She didn't look into Holly's eyes; all she saw was this poor struggling body—not our baby's sweet soul!"

She shuddered out a wrenching sob.

"I should pity that woman—she deserves pity. But if I could make her writhe like Holly when she's crying, tense from all that's wrong inside—I would, I would! Why didn't I tell her how I feel: 'Get out of my house and away from my baby!' Oh, it's horrible to grow up poor and never feel that you can tell people off! If she had condemned you and me, I could have taken it, but why can't she see Holly kindly, with compassion, and see that we're only trying to make her comfortable?"

Dad coughed. He'd turned fifty-one years old the week before, and his smoker's hack was a little worse lately. He put his arm around Mama and spoke firmly.

"Joyce—you're doing the right thing. We're doing right. The Lord can take her if He needs to. But the Lord saw fit to let us care for her while she's here, and we will."

My eyes opened. Usually, it was Mama who talked about the Lord—this time, it was Dad!

"Wayne, she's struggling. Her heart is working harder."

"And Doc Melcher says...?"

"He does his best, but he admits there's not much he can do." The bed springs squeaked as Mama handed Holly to Dad.

"What about that doctor in Idaho Falls who was so

good the night she was born?" Dad asked. "His name was Lashell or something like that."

"He's a pediatrician. You said he was kind. And he knew that heart doctor in Salt Lake. Oh, Wayne, let's take her to him!" Mama sounded excited. "I'll send Brenda to Teton, and she can call and make an appointment."

Dad sighed. "I hope he doesn't mind if we can't pay him for a while."

Andrea and Shanan busted into Mama's room with wild roses for her. I curled up in my spot. *We're a loud, messy family. When Dad yells, it echoes off the roof. We kids argue like crazy. We don't always make it to church, and we aren't sealed in the temple. But we love Holly. And we*—my tears flowed, and I knew it was true of me, too, despite my jealousy—*we would never "let Holly go."*

I slept through the tapping of the typewriter that night. It would be fifty years before I knew that Mama wrote to Dr. Lechelt to prepare him for their appointment. Somehow Mama trusted Dr. Lechelt, and she unburdened her heart to him. Her own children must never know the terrible truth about Holly's chromosome deficiency, but she needed to share her feelings with someone. As she typed, she hit the "dash" key often and hard—every dash was a slit in her heart.

Shaping her tears into words eased Mama's soul. The last words of the letter were: "…the most important thing Holly has taught us is to approach life a day at a time, loving her and enjoying her, grateful for whatever time we have her. We derive comfort from the fact that we sort of gave her over to God, so now we have only to watch over her the best we can while He lets her stay with us."

Dr. Lechelt later suggested that Mama's letter and methods for the care of ill infants be edited and submitted for publication, but sadly, that never happened. If it had, many parents would have been blessed by Mama's wisdom, which she learned at her mother's knee and perfected in days and nights taking care of Holly.

Dr. Ronald K. Lechelt and his wife, Nancy, in 2017. He saved Mama's letters to him, and a copy of his reply to her, and mailed them to the Nelson family. He wood-burned this quote into driftwood: "The purpose of man is to be present for the future of others and not be suffocated by their presence."—Dag Hammarskjöld He said he found this to be true in his career as a pediatrician, and it is excellent advice for all medical caregivers who must care for patients while guarding their own hearts. We are thankful that he, and other medical friends, have been present for Holly and our family over the years.

Mama's Letter To Dr. Ronald K. Lechelt

Parts of this letter appeared in a previous chapter. It is shared here in its entirety. Items in [ ] are clarifying additions.

Mrs. F. Wayne Nelson

Star route, Newdale, Ida.

July 14, 1967

Dr. Ronald K. Lechelt
Specialist in Pediatrics
9 at Oxford Dr.
Idaho Falls, Ida.

Dear Doctor,

We are so very grateful you gave us an appointment for our baby, especially when we have been so careless about sending the payment for the first time you examined her.

We thought that perhaps if we'd send you a letter telling all we know of the findings of the other doctors, it would save precious time in your office.

She has so many problems – – never at any time has any doctor given us any hope for her; but she has lived three and one-half months now and has wrapped herself around the heart –strings of this family until we just feel that we must learn from somewhere if we're doing all for her that can be done.

Her heart is greatly enlarged, her left ear deformed, her fingers clenched into fists, and her legs crossed most of the time. She cannot focus her eyes and they are crossed; her right eye sort of lags shut. Her head may be shaped a little different and there seems to be a little opening out from the soft spot in her head where the skull bones just barely missed joining. The thing that gives us hope for her mind is that wonderful left eye, there seems to be so much intelligence shining from it. She turns her head to see people, especially her Dad, when she hears a voice. She watches our lips and purses hers up and tries to smile.

Maybe it will be best if I go back to the beginning and tell you all we have learned, which isn't much.

After you examined her the evening of April 7, [6,] her father and brother arrived in Salt Lake with her at 2 A.M., she was put directly into the intensive care unit [of Primary Children's Hospital.] She was only kept in there about 36 hours.

Holly spent 20 days in Salt Lake City. She was checked every way possible, and they told us there was scarcely any chance she could live.

We were able to see Dr. Veasy, the heart specialist, for only a short time. He told us, "Your baby has other troubles than her heart." He referred us to Dr. S. who had been on duty when Wayne registered the baby in the hospital and had charge of her case. Four doctors had conducted tests on her: Dr. S., Dr. Veasy, Dr. C. and Dr. R.

Dr. C. told us that in every case he had seen where a little ear was deformed, the kidneys would cease to function. Dr. R. had just a few minutes to speak to us also—he said, "She cannot live, it seems, and really the most tragic thing will be if she does."

The findings which Dr. S. presented to us were heartbreaking. She has a chromosome deficiency. (When I remember now that interview, it seems to me that possibly this Doctor had come to like Wayne, in those first few days, while I was still in the hospital at Ashton, and that when he was faced with the duty of telling us so tragic a truth, he was brusque and blunt and so quick about it that we were left stunned and trembling. I remember that he called the baby 'it.')

He said, "It has everything in the book wrong with it. You can tell that just by looking at it. Even if it didn't have, as Dr. Veasy records it here, "a heart that is incompatible with life'—first one thing and then another would go wrong with it, its mind, its liver, its kidneys, none of its organs will function properly. Now you folks have other children, I met your fine son (this was our boy, who had just returned from service overseas, and drove to Salt Lake, while Wayne kept the oxygen on the baby, that first night). I suggest you consider them-do not love and fondle this child and give it the will to live, because if it does, it will be tragic."

At first, all we could do is blame ourselves for giving life and suffering to our child. Our prayer was "Dear Lord, we give this tiny one into thy keeping, only help us that we may do nothing to make her suffer more."

A few days later, a pediatrician from back East was at the hospital, his diagnosis was the same as the Salt Lake doctors'. It was after this that they decided we could bring her home, if we would equip our home so we could keep her in oxygen.

We appreciated the nurses at the Primary Hospital more than we can say. It seemed to us that they, just as we, could not keep the last part of Dr. S.'s admonition "not to love and fondle this precious child." It wasn't that anyone wanted to keep her here if she must suffer, it just somehow seems that every living thing deserves love and respect as one of God's creations. A loving and just God will surely take her to him in spite of all we can do to make her stay here easier. As for considering the other children, what can make better individuals of them than loving this little one in spite of all her difficulties?

In Salt Lake they advised us to take her to our family doctor, Dr. W. L. Melcher in Ashton. Dr. Melcher and Dr. Krueger of Ashton both advised us to keep her in oxygen whenever she turned a little blue. He had us bring her to him each week and each of the first few times he seemed amazed that she had lived through the week.

These two articles have helped us so much, although we realize Holly's case is probably more serious than either. Still, many of the statements give us some sort of hope to live by. We thought perhaps you would like to glance through them, if you haven't already read them. For you have probably had cases similar to these. (We'd like to get them back if possible.)

Thank you.

Sincerely, Mrs. F. Wayne Nelson
Star route, Newdale, Idaho

Enclosures:

- *Two articles [They have been lost; titles unknown.]*
- *Handwritten Progress Report*
- *Questions*
- *Things we've learned from Holly*

We thought that perhaps if we'd send you a letter telling, all we know, of the findings of the other doctors, it would save precious time in your office.

She has so many problems--never at any time has any Doctor given us any hope for her; but she has lived three and a half months now and has wrapped herself around the heart-strings of this family until we just feel that we must learn from somewhere if we're doing all for her that can be done.

Mama poured out her feelings in her letter to Dr. Lechelt, a portion of which is shared in this scanned image.

PROGRESS REPORT OF HOLLY JOYCE NELSON

Daughter of Wayne and Joyce Nelson Newdale, Idaho

Date:	Weight:	Comments:
Born Apr. 6, 1967	6 lb. 11 oz	
Apr. 13		*In Salt Lake City*
Apr. 20	*5 lb.*	"
Apr. 27	*5 lb. 4 oz.*	
May 4	*5 lb. 8 oz.*	*Brought her home - In oxygen almost all the time*
May 11	*5 lb. 4 oz.*	*Is listless—feeding her with eyedropper each hour. Has enema at 10 a.m. and 10 p.m.*
May 18	*5 lb. 6 oz.*	*Finally got her to drink from bottle w/ preemie nipple*
May 25	*5 lb. 11 oz.*	*Has pan baths – relaxes her so she can sleep, and eats every two hours*
June 1	*5 lb. 14 oz.*	
June 8	*6 lb. 6 oz.*	*She's two months old now*

June 15	*6 lb. 9 oz.*	*Cry stronger – watches other children of family*
June 22	*6 lbs. 12 oz.*	*Very responsive – turns to hear voices, sleeps well*
June 29	*6 lb. 15 oz.*	*Eats quite well*
July 6	*6 lb. 11 oz.*	*Has fever – temperature 104 Bathe her every few hours to cool her, sponge her to keep her cool. Stay up nights to keep check on her.* [Dr. Melcher said she nearly had pneumonia at this time.]
July 13	*6 lb. 8 oz.*	
July 20	*6 lb. 5 oz.*	*The fever came back. Seems to have bad cold.*
July 27	*?*	*Giving her ____________ Doctor's prescription and a small amount of Aspirin and neosynephrine nose drops*

May 4 "	5 lbs. 08 oz.	In oxygen almost all the time— has enema at 10 A.M. and 1 A.P.M.
" 11 "	5 lbs. 04 oz.	Is listless—feeding her with eyedropper " " each hour
" 18 "	5 lbs. 06 oz.	Finally got her to drink from bottle with
" 25 "	5 lb. 11 oz.	preemie nipple.— Has pan baths—relaxes her
June 1 "	5 lb. 14 oz.	so she can sleep.— Eats every two hours.
" 8 "	6 lbs. 06 oz.	—She's two months old now.
" 15 "	6 lbs. 09 oz.	cry stronger—watches other children of family.
" 22 "	6 lbs. 13 oz.	very responsive—turns to hear voices—sleeps
" 29 "	6 lbs. 15 oz.	well. Eats quite well.
July 6 "	6 lbs. 11 oz.	Has fever—temperature 104 Bathe her every few hours
" 13 "	6 lbs. 08 oz.	—to cool her sponge her to
" 20 "	6 lbs. 05 oz.	keep her cool stay up nights to keep check on her.
" 27 "	?	The fever came back seems to have bad cold giving her Doctor's perscription Small amount of Asprin — Neo Synephrine Nose Dropps

Mama's record of Holly's weight, interventions, and health are shown in this scanned image; Mama did everything detailed in the enclosures as she cared for Holly. Dr. Lechelt was so impressed that he asked Mama's permission to send her ideas to a magazine for publication. This never happened, and it is unfortunate, for her loving methods would have been a blessing to parents of ill children.

Questions

- *What harm does being in oxygen constantly do?*
- *She is so inactive; will gentle exercises hurt her?*
- *Have you known other cases similar to Holly's?*
- *Is there something we can do for her that we haven't thought of?*
- *Has any child with like ailments lived very long?*
- *How much pain does she suffer? She seems to have painful cramps.*
- *Will she be able to learn some things? It seems to us that she turns when she hears a dog bark, or different voices.—*

Things we've learned from Holly:

Ways to get a nervous baby to take her bottle:

Let them know they are loved.

A. By snuggling their little face with yours so that it will resemble breast-feeding for them.

B. Let other children talk to them, while snuggling them safely against you.

C. You and other children who happen to be around, sing happy lullabies. This gives children a chance to do something to show their love and tenderness for a baby too ill and fragile to be held or played with by them.

D. Rock them and croon to them. (If they must be kept in bassinet with oxygen, reach in, hold their little hand, just let them know you are there and want them to eat.)

E. Almost all babies like the sound of a man's voice, especially Dad's. It really helps relax them.

When a baby is weak—an enema, then a bath in warm water, relaxes them and lets them sleep without giving them so much medicine. She seems to appreciate a brisk rub (brisk but gentle) with a soft towel to pep up circulation.

Baby powder may make it harder for a baby in this condition to breathe.

A rub with baby lotion helps a great deal for a baby who isn't able to be active in this hot weather.

Olive oil has proved to be the best rub. Even with the constant enemas (two every 24-hour day) she has never had a diaper rash.

A vaporizer, used all the time the oxygen is, seems to help the patient's skin from dehydrating.

The four white sides of the bassinet can get to seeming like a prison to a baby, so if a way can be devised to still get the oxygen to them and yet let them watch the activity going on around them, they will be happier and learn about their 'limited' world faster. – – – This can work two ways, though, for when a baby is sleepy and tired, maybe even turning a bit blue, then the bassinet becomes their sanctuary.

The time taken to coax water or juices (so far, at 3 1/2 months, orange juice is all she has kept down) is well worthwhile for it keeps them from dehydrating.

Rice (baby cereal) and banana flakes are the only two foods other than formula she has kept down; we find it best to feed just a teaspoonful at a time, one or the other, each time she has formula.

I guess the most important thing Holly has taught us is to approach life a day at a time, loving her and enjoying her, grateful for whatever time we have her. We derive comfort from the fact that we sort of gave her over to God, so now we have only to watch over her the best we can while He lets her stay with us.

Like many Idaho families in the 1960s, we relied on Mother Nature for much of our diet. We harvested trout, deer, elk, and game birds for protein; and huckleberries, chokecherries, and sarvis berries for taste and fiber, not to mention for pies, jams, and jellies. Here we are showing off a "mess" of fish in 1960. Left to right: Brenda, Jeanne, Dad holding Andrea, with me and Rex in front. Our wood pile and coal pile are on the hill behind us, with the watering trough for stock on the far right. The structure with a ladder is our well.

The Fat Of The Land

Holly was sick for a few days, and Dr. Melcher said she nearly had pneumonia.

Our 4-H Club presented its yearly Community Picnic and program for Clementsville farm families on July 19. Brenda and I acted out a skit about a paranoid man who thought he looked like a plate of spaghetti and meatballs. His doctor told him to repeat, "I do not look like a plate of spaghetti and meatballs." An angry customer threw a plate of spaghetti and meatballs at someone else, and it landed on his head while he yelled his slogan. It was hilarious, in our humble opinions.

Bugging ended. Pine beetle larvae turn into adults and fly to new trees by mid-July, so there's no point in spraying any more goop. Rex paid me forty-two dollars, and I retired from milking.

***

Tuesday, July 25, 1967

CLEMENTSVILLE

Dad made a pot of beans. They were good, but we were tired of beans.

"Debbie, take Andrea and Shanan to the shop, and bring back my big Phillips screwdriver," Dad said after supper. He was unlocking the gun cabinet and pulling out his 30.06 Springfield rifle.

Something's up—there are Phillips screwdrivers in his pickup and in the house. Why all three of us?

I asked Andrea, "Do you know what a Phillips screwdriver looks like?"

"Sure! Remember when I took the screen door off?" That was one of the few times Andrea got in trouble, but she put the door back on with a little help.

"Good! I didn't know that when I was seven. You're smart. You and Shanan go to the shop and find the biggest one you can for Dad, all right?"

She grinned, and they took off running.

I climbed into the back of the pickup and huddled under a tarp, glad that it was one of Dad's cleaner tarps. Before the little girls got back, Dad, Bruce, Brenda, and Rex got in the cab. Dad took the upper road along the canyon rim, heading two miles south toward the mountain.

When Dad cut the engine, the guys spilled out and loaded their rifles. I stayed still, unsure when to make my presence known.

"Brenda, drive the truck home. Until I get the car brakes bled and fixed, it's Mama's only vehicle in case Holly needs help. We'll walk back if we don't connect, and Bruce will come get the truck if we do," Dad said.

I popped out like a chisler from its hole.

Dad cussed. "What're you doing? Had to see what was going on, huh? Okay, get over here. Maybe you'll learn something that'll help you—*after* you take Hunters Safety Course next spring. On summer days, elk hang around that spring that bubbles up near the Hugh Davis cabin. Go with Rex, and make a loop through the canyon bottom."

Dad settled himself against a tree near the road. "Bruce, circle north, and see what you stir up."

We walked down an old dugway, built with stones placed by pioneer hands, to the Davis cabin, rotting into the grass and fern. We watched where we stepped in the darkening canyon bottom.

Two shadows emerged from the wallow—an old cow elk and a spike bull. I gasped. "Walk toward 'em," Rex whispered. "We're upwind, they can't smell us."

The elk noticed us and trotted up the dugway, straight toward Dad. Seconds later the 30.06 fired, once, and again.

"That was Dad's finishing shot," Rex said as we hurried up the dugway.

Moments before, those elk had slurped water in the seep. Now one lay dead, its open eyes glinting in the sun setting across the upland.

A lump choked my throat.

"Feeling bad?" Dad asked. I nodded. "Every animal and every person on earth has to die sometime. A mountain lion might have killed this elk, or it might have starved if there wasn't enough winter forage. A hunter might've killed it this fall. We need meat, and we appreciate this animal."

He put his arms out, and I was swallowed in his hug. "It's hard, isn't it, honey?"

Hiding in the truck was the stupidest trick I've ever pulled, I thought as I nodded.

Bruce walked up, saying, "Dad, if I get the truck, we can load up before it gets too late."

"Yeah, go get it. Come on, Rex, let's gut him out."

Rex pulled his knife out of its scabbard, and Dad asked me, "You got a knife?"

"No."

"Didn't think so. Lucky you."

I watched. I *was* lucky—when Mama asked Brenda and me to cut up chickens, I wiggled out of it by doing Brenda's dishes for a week. I hated blood as much as she hated dishes. My head spun from the odor of warm blood and guts, and the thought that hunting season wouldn't open for weeks. *Dad had poached.*

They gutted the elk steadily, eyeing the failing daylight as the moon rose in the east.

"Coyotes, foxes, and crows'll eat good tonight," Rex said, tossing entrails into the bushes.

"Cut the heart and liver free, and put them in that flour sack, son," Dad said. Rex sighed.

"What is it, son?"

"What if we get caught?"

Dad straightened, coughed, and spat. "*We* won't get caught. If a game warden comes, *I'll* get caught. You didn't pull the trigger, and you're not at fault. I wouldn't have done it if we hadn't lost so much meat when the power to the freezer went off. Grocery money's tight."

Rex got back to work.

A rifle cracked half a mile away.

"Bruce must have blasted the head off of a pheasant," Dad grunted.

Finally, Dad stood up. "We've got to get this carcass into the spud cellar tonight. Bruce is taking forever. I'll finish, and you two head home and stir him up."

Rex and I took the quickest way home, the way Bruce had gone, dropping back into the canyon.

I'd missed Rex. We usually played together all summer.

"Hey, are you glad to be home?"

"Yeah." He was quiet. "When we came in after the last day of bugging, Mama was busy with the baby...." He paused. "Almost too busy to give me a smile or a hug."

"Sometimes it's hard with Holly. So much work to do, and Mama's always tied up with her."

He sighed. "I've been gone so much; it feels like I hardly know Holly. I'm ashamed of how much I wanted a baby brother. Mama let me feed her a bottle today."

The moon was sliding from full to half, and its light spread over the sagebrush hill to our right, but on our dark path under the aspen, we watched for long grass that would trip us or branches that could scrape an arm or leg.

I cleared my throat. "So—Dad poached tonight."

"Yeah, we poached. So what? Driving up here tonight, Dad told us a story from the Depression when deer were eating Grandpa Nelson's spring wheat and haystacks. Grandpa didn't shoot any deer, but a neighbor shot two, and gave one to them, and they were glad to get it. They were low on meat."

I snorted, and he got defensive. "Well, back then, wardens turned a blind eye sometimes. Especially when there was a large herd of wildlife that might have a hard time finding food in the winter. Especially when there were hungry kids to be fed."

"It's poaching."

"Shut up, you little sneak. You can't even hunt yet, so why'd you hide in the truck? Dad's doing what he has to do, and Mama, too!" He walked faster, and I had to trot to keep up.

"We're coming to the clearing where I shot my first deer last fall," Rex said.

"Go ahead, change the subject. *Dad poached*." I was right for once, and I wasn't going to let him forget it.

He turned on me. "The elk are eating grass in our canyon when they can't eat Uncle Henry's grain. It's like we've fattened 'em up. I've got all the respect in the world for game laws, but we need meat now, not two months from now, when hunting season opens."

A black cloud scudded over the moon, covering the open hillside in shadow and darkening Rex's clearing. A night bird called. At the head of the draw to the east was the burial spot of a pioneer family's son; Mama said the boy had died in a measles epidemic. Rex called it "Rigor Mortis's grave." Their cabin had rotted away, but lilacs bloomed every spring on the bush they planted over the grave, and that bush made me think of that little child, not some old codger named Rigor Mortis.

A twig cracked under underfoot, and I jumped.

"I was thinking about how we're not very scared of the dark at the farm," I said. The truth was that my first hunting trip—bloody, moonlit, and impromptu—had made me jittery.

"You're not afraid of Rigor Mortis's ghost—ooowwwweee?" He grabbed my arm.

"Don't touch me! Your hands have blood n' guts on 'em. I'm not scared of ghosts, not that little boy buried up there. Cemeteries, even one little grave, feel peaceful. But wolves, mountain lions, bears—yeah, they scare me. Have you ever seen any of those around here?"

Dark shadows loomed in the trees. Predators might lurk nearby.

"Once, looking for a Christmas tree, Bruce and I saw a bear over on Canyon Creek, headed for his winter den. Dad saw a sow bear and cubs in this canyon one early spring. They usually move into the timber before May. Oh! What's that?"

A large, humped form stood in the clearing to our left. Shadowy, but maybe...*a black bear, head down, snuffling along the ground?*

"Run, Rex! We smell like dead elk!" I screamed. Long grass tore my feet and ankles as I pelted down the dark path. The odor of guts wafted sharp and strong into my nose. I looked over my shoulder, thinking I felt a bear's hot breath on my neck. When I turned around, something brushed my face—I was bumped, hard, by a large body covered in thick fur, matted with fresh blood, swinging from a dead tree.

"EEEeeee—Unnnnhuhhhh!" I pushed it—whatever it was—away. It swung back toward me.

Brenda harvested this whitetail spike in 1968 or 1969. Dad and Mama made sure we attended Hunter Education classes and understood gun safety before we were allowed to handle rifles. Dad was extremely strict about gun safety. We always bought hunting and fishing licenses and tags, and hunted in the proper seasons, with the exception of the story detailed here.

Waiting

I ducked, and Rex grabbed the furry body before it hit me again.

A mule deer carcass, split open to cool, dangled from the broken branch of an aspen stub.

"Bruce must have shot this deer! That's the shot we heard!" Rex said.

"S-S-So what was back there? It looked like a bear!" I sunk to the ground, shaking.

"That was a chokecherry thicket!" Rex laughed. "You've seen that bush in the clearing for years in daylight. The look on your face—I didn't know you could run so fast!"

He gave me a hand up. I looked back up the canyon. The thing wasn't a bear, and it wasn't chasing me. It *was* a chokecherry bush!

Rex punched my arm. I giggled, and then we both

laughed.

The headlights of the pickup bounced toward us through the dark.

Bruce pulled up, and Rex told the tale of my "bear attack" while we loaded the deer on the tarp and drove to the top of the canyon.

Dad dozed against an aspen tree. "Did you shoot a pheasant, Bruce?" he mumbled when we pulled up.

"Nope! Look in the truck. When this young buck wandered out of the bushes, I thought, 'Why not? It's been a long two years in France with no hunting.'"

"You young knot-head! Now there's more work. Venison AND elk meat!" He grinned. "All right—we needed meat, and we got it, and we're grateful. Let's load the elk!"

Light from the kitchen splashed onto the lawn, a grateful sight after hours in the dark. Dad dropped me at the house. He and the boys would hang the game behind the closed doors of the old potato cellar which doubled as Dad's shop. It was the coolest place to dry-age the meat during July.

The red and white kitchen clock pointed to midnight. Mama was finishing dishes that I had been asked to wash.

"I wondered where you'd gone," she said.

"I sneaked into the truck. I didn't know they'd go up the canyon and, um, shoot an elk."

"Daddy didn't want you little girls to know, but I guess you're not a little girl anymore." She dried her hands.

"Rex and I spooked it up to Dad to get shot," I said, and sobs I'd been holding in overflowed. Mama held me tight and murmured, "There, there." After I blew my nose, she told me about the first time she saw an animal die—when her Daddy was killing hogs for the winter, and one of her favorite pigs had his throat cut.

"It's hard for me to see animals die, but never as hard as that first time."

"Dad poached," I hiccupped.

"I'm sorry, honey. It's the first time he's done that, and he feels bad about it. We need meat."

"What if other people heard the shots? Oh, and Bruce shot a deer," I said. Mama raised an eyebrow.

"He did! Well…we're so remote that there's not much chance that anyone heard any shots."

I crawled into bed next to Andrea, and she murmured, "Daddy didn't need a screwdriver! Where did you go?"

"Dad shot an elk up the canyon, and we'll have liver and onions tomorrow," I said. She smiled, and I did, too. Tomorrow Dad would fry fresh elk liver with plenty of onions in bacon grease, seasoned just right. When the rest of the meat had aged, Dad would cut it into roasts and steaks and grind the scraps into burger. We would wrap and label the meat and fill the freezer. Again and again, we'd fill our bellies. We might have to charge things at the Merc, but not chicken, pork, or beef.

Sometimes death has to happen. I drifted to sleep.

***

Monday, July 31, 1967

TETON

Brenda and I ran Mama's errands, but we collapsed at the Teton house. With its stone walls and tall spruce trees, it was a cool, dark retreat from summer's heat and a return to civilization—television. When the phone rang, Brenda beat me to it; she always did.

"Thanks, we'll be right over. Bye." She picked up the car keys. "Grandma Rackham saw the car here and made our supper. We better go get it and get back to the farm."

"Let me finish *As the World Turns.*"

"We've wasted too much time." She turned the television off, and I grumbled all the way to the car.

Grandma Rackham asked about Holly, exchanging a look with Brenda, who shook her head slightly.

"She's doing better every day. Mama says she's gained weight!" I said.

"That sounds—good." Her words hung in the air. She added, "Now girls, remember that the hardest part of anything is waiting. Your Mama's waiting. Be good to her, help her all you can." My gut twisted.

"Thanks so much for this supper. It smells good," Brenda said. "We'll bring your dish back next time we come to Teton. We'd better go, we've messed around too long already."

"What's Mama waiting for?" I asked as Brenda started the car. "Mama's busy every second. I don't think she's waiting for anything."

"I dunno. She's probably waiting for *us* right now. Grandma's right, we need to help Mama more." She stepped on the gas. "Turn on the radio. Let's listen to KUPI while we have good reception." She was hedging.

I stared out the window. Sprinklers fed by canal water sprayed blossoming potato crops along Highway 33. We rumbled over Canyon Creek bridge where tumbling water fed lush green bushes far below. Uncle Henry's grain was nearly ripe. *What is Mama waiting for? Everything is alive. Even Holly. Doctors said Holly would die, but she has lived.*

She was living when we walked in the door. Mama was giving her a bath in the kitchen with Shanan and Andrea helping. When Holly was born, I worried a lot about her dying, but it seemed like God had blessed her. Keeping her alive was a lot of work for Mama, but I remembered the story of Isaac and Abraham. *Maybe God will put a sheep in the thicket for Holly. And for Mama and Dad. Maybe Holly will grow up.*

Mama put us to work so she could feed Holly and get her to sleep. While Brenda kneaded bread, I washed dishes. She whispered, "Debbie, there's something you need to know. When Holly gains weight, it makes her heart work harder."

I stared out the window at Andrea and Shanan playing in the sandbox next to the swing.

"So, gaining weight isn't good for her."

"No."

My tears fell into the dishwater, and Brenda patted me with a floury hand.

***

Thursday, August 3, 1967

CLEMENTSVILLE

"Mama, I'm hot, and hungry, and sick of everything," I groaned.

"I hear the truck coming; the guys are back from fishing. We'll fry some fish."

"It better be fast. I'm dying." Using the excuse that I was having my period, I'd stayed home and sulked rather than hike the steep narrows of the Teton River on a hot day with Dad, Rex, and Andrea. I had worked myself into a toxic mess of self-pity, hunger, and adolescent hormone spikes.

"I went fishing, and I'm only seven!" Andrea bounced into the kitchen.

Rex dumped a creel full of fish into the dishpan.

"I caught those three!" Andrea squealed, pointing.

"Big deal," I grumped. "I bet Dad hooked 'em and all you did was pull them in."

"I did, too, catch them! I did! Daddy broke the rule that he wouldn't take a kid fishing 'til they're eight years old, and he took me! And I caught grasshoppers for bait."

"No, you didn't!" I protested. "Kids your age are no good at that. Remember, before you left, I caught most of them, you caught about five." I was better than her at sneaking up on a grasshopper and grabbing it, snatching a handful of grass as well, and performing the tricky task of opening a Prince Albert tobacco can a tiny crack and forcing the grasshopper in, without letting other hoppers out. Grasshoppers don't like it. They spit "tobacco juice" on your hands.

"I did my best to catch 'em, and you *wanted* to help me!"

"Well, go on being *so proud* of yourself for reeling in fish that Dad caught!"

"She did all right for a kid her age," Rex said. "She climbed the ledges like a trooper, and she reeled them in. Not a one flipped off the hook."

"She's a prodigy, but don't expect me to stand around singing *Kumbaya* with the two of you!" I yelled.

I stormed into Mama and Dad's room and flopped onto their bed, emotions boiling. I was stuck at home when I wanted to be goofing around with Marilyn. The day before, Brenda and I had attended 4-H activities in Driggs, and Mama had allowed Brenda to stay with Uncle Ern's family, so she could earn money picking peas with our cousins. All day I'd hatched plots to get myself over the mountain range to Marilyn's house.

Mama brought Holly in.

"Mama, could Dad drive me to Uncle Ern's tonight so I can pick peas? The farmer hires twelve-year-olds; he hired Marilyn."

"No, honey, I need your help." Mama rubbed lotion on Holly's feet.

"Dad could bring Brenda back, and she could help you. I'll be in junior high school, and I need to earn money for school clothes!"

"You earned money milking Swiss Miss. Honey, can you mix and warm Holly's bottle for her? And heat the frying pan to cook the fish?"

"Sure, *if* you let me go to Marilyn's!"

"That's not how it works!"

"You never let me have fun! You don't care that all the kids at school will think I'm a dope in hand-me-downs. All you care about is Holly!"

"You know that's not true!"

Holly whimpered nervously.

"It is true!" I sobbed. I pounded Mama's pillow and yelled, "I don't matter to anybody! You don't love me as much as you love Holly!"

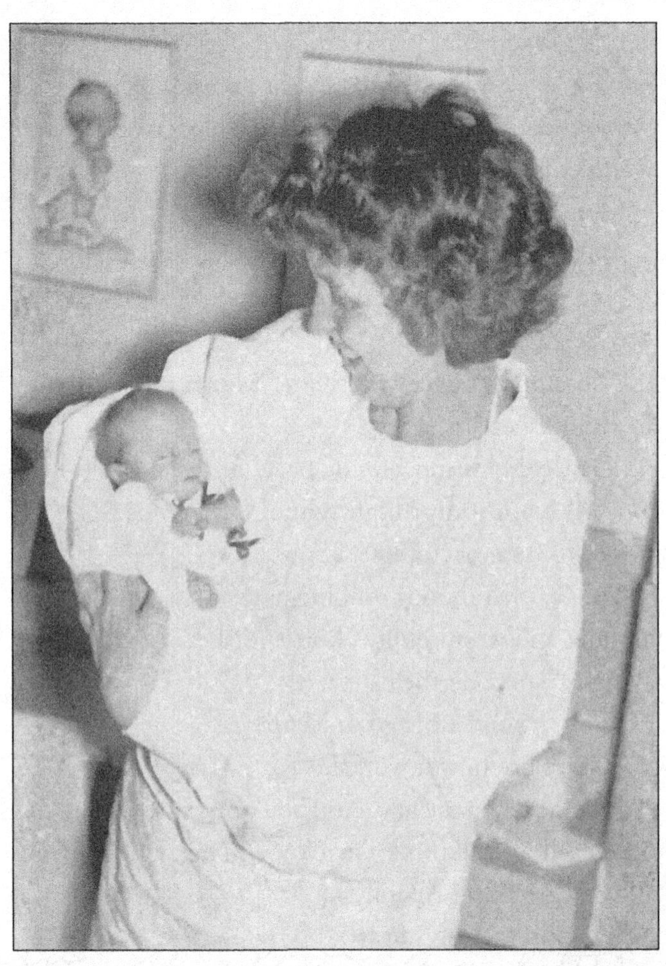

Mama radiated joy when she cuddled Holly at Primary Children's Hospital. It's a blessing that someone took photos of them there because we do not have many photos of Mama with Holly. She was always in the background, encouraging others to be photographed with the precious baby, often while taking the photographs herself.

The Terror of Thunder

I sobbed and thrashed as Mama warmed Holly's bottle and pushed my legs aside to sit on the bed and croon to Holly. She was *I-G-N-O-R-I-N-G* me, and it drove me crazy. My sobs subsided, but I hadn't given up. I started to speak, but Mama beat me to it.

"Debbie, if you imagined that your summer would consist of overnight trips to Marilyn's and dragging Main with Brenda, you can see that's not happening. I understand that you're mad at the world about Holly's troubles. I'm mad, too, and I cry about it. Our lives have changed. We have a very sick baby girl, and we all need to help her. You've worked hard taking care of Holly and helping so I can take care of her. Thank you." She could not have been kinder, nor more firm, as she looked past my red eyes and into my soul. "But you'll need to do more."

I need to do more? I don't want to do more. Then that other voice—the Holy Ghost—whispered: *You can do more, and it will be all right. You'll see.*

The scent of sizzling butter wafted in. I could hear Dad and Rex talking about how well fish were biting in the fabled Big Hole. Mama handed me a wad of toilet paper. I wiped my eyes and stood. Not angry. Still. Peaceful, even. *I can do more.*

"Would you wash your face and hands, and feed this little one?"

"Sure," I said. From the bed, Mama reached out an arm and clumsily squeezed me around the legs.

Tomorrow Brenda and our cousins would flirt with cute boys in the Teton Valley pea fields while I lugged baskets of clothes to the clothesline. Tomorrow Rex would help Bruce pack up bug camp and celebrate with a hamburger and fries in town while I tended the little girls and milked Miss. Tomorrow I would help at home.

Today I would eat fresh trout that smelled sublime—as soon as Holly finished her bottle.

***

Most days, I wrote in my diary that Holly was "better" or "doing well" because I asked Mama, and that's what she said. On July 31, I wrote *Holly better and cries a lot*—even though that was contradictory. On August

1, I wrote, *Mama and Dad took Holly to Dr. Lashell [sic] She weighs seven lb. six oz. and is doing well.* On August 3, I recorded: *Holly worse.* On August 4: *Mama thought Holly bad.*

***

Friday, August 4, 1967

CLEMENTSVILLE

"Debbie! Dress the baby!" I couldn't discern the subtle change in Holly that made Mama speak so sharply as she jerked her nylons on.

Thunder rumbled, and rain splattered on the window.

At four months, Holly was the size of a newborn, and I'd dressed her many times: secured her cloth diaper with two pink duck-headed diaper pins, eased on an undershirt, and carefully pulled plastic pants over her stiff legs.

Andrea sat next to us and softly sang "Hello, Holly." Holly seemed to listen.

"Can she wear her rosebud dress with white lace panties?" I asked.

Mama threw me a clean nightgown. I frowned. Usually, we dressed Holly in her best for a trip to the doctor.

On my lap, Holly gazed—her left eye as wide as I had ever seen it—as if cataloguing images of blue and white curtains, flapping in the wind and Mama's back as she rummaged in her closet.

Then, for several seconds, Holly looked into my eyes. I memorized her liquid blue eyes, one nearly closed; her soft dark hair; her mouth pinched into a worried, pain-filled O; her tiny rosebud-enfolded left ear, and her perfect right ear. Holly: my sweet baby sister.

Hail rattled on the window. I swaddled Holly and laid her in the bassinet. Mama wound up the oxygen tube and tipped the heavy oxygen cylinder to one side, then we rolled it across the bedroom and kitchen. We lifted it down a step into the front porch and across the threshold, rolled it a few feet further, then, grunting, muscled it down the six cement steps in front of the house.

Stung with hailstones, we rolled the tank down the terrace and settled it on the back floor of the Ford Fairlane. Thunder rumbled as we rushed back into the house for Holly, the bassinet, and the diaper bag.

"Andrea, watch Shanan when she wakes up." Mama covered the bassinet with a baby quilt. "Debbie's going with me to get Daddy at Uncle Lester's, then she'll come back."

"Mama, I don't want to be alone! I'm scared of thunder!" Andrea wailed.

"You can do it. You can do hard things." Mama was firm.

I knelt on the front seat, leaning into the back. This way, I could keep the oxygen tube closer to Holly's nostrils. Mama pulled out as fast as she dared on the muddy road. Hailstones peppered the car.

Through sheets of hail, I glimpsed Andrea's forlorn face at the kitchen window.

I gripped the back of the seat as we jounced toward a brimming quagmire. Even Dad got stuck in this gooey dry farm mud.

"Honey, pray!" Mama said.

It was a loud, eyes-open prayer. "Dear Father in Heaven, please help us not get stuck. Please help Holly breathe. Please..." I couldn't hear myself over the hail. Mama hit a puddle at the right speed, gripping the wheel, willing the tires to maintain traction. The tires spun, but we didn't sink. We made it to the gate.

Pounded with icy hail that soaked my clothes, I opened and closed the barbed wire gate at top speed. Mama took a deep breath and gunned toward the miry hole around the corner. Holly's lips were blue. She was sucking for air.

We hit the puddle and spun. *If we get stuck, I'll have to run for Dad and Uncle Lester, three miles away, to pull us out with a tractor. Mama and Holly will have to wait in the car.* Lightning flashed, and thunder cracked right above us. Mama prayed, and her answer came quickly, for she hit the slick spot just right, and we labored through and up the hill.

We prayed again as we approached the next big puddle. Mama's hands gripped the wheel, and her arms see-sawed, feeling for the high spots in the ruts, back and forth, back and forth, finding traction. Somehow, we got to the other side.

Lightning split the sky and thunder roared at the same moment. Holly's nostrils tightened. She couldn't cry; she was struggling too hard to breathe, fighting the air pressure of the storm. *If I was Mama, I'd push the gas to the floor!* We topped the hill above the biggest mud hole.

Water poured down the hills into a raging Timothy Creek at the end of our canyon. The cloudburst had carved channels in a barley field, dumping slushy water in our path.

"Dear Lord, please help us through, help Mama, help Holly, help..." I didn't know if it was Mama or me praying. Mama's face was rigid, her hands bone-white on the steering wheel.

Our tires hit the icy, muddy ruts and labored gamely for a few seconds. Then they spun, ever so slightly. If you hit the middle of a mud hole and lose traction, it's over. We were stuck.

"NO! NO! She needs a doctor!" Mama cried. The car was sinking into a current, and the mud hole was deeper and more treacherous than when I helped push Brenda out of it.

"Easy—less gas. Help me, Lord. Help!" Mama groaned. I held the oxygen tube very close to Holly's nose. It didn't seem to help; she was turning blue.

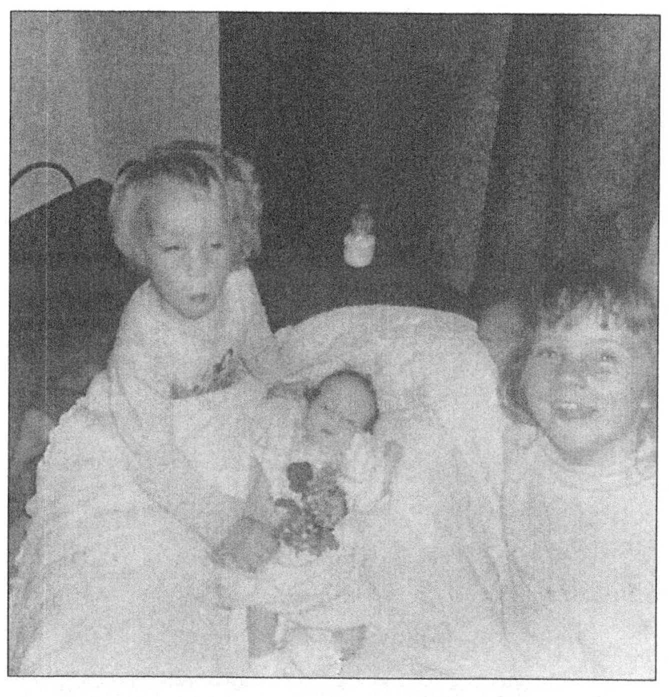

Shanan (left) and Andrea (right) loved Holly. Mama vigilantly helped them enjoy their baby sister in ways that didn't hurt her. When Andrea had the idea that we should sing all kinds of songs to Holly, it gave the rest of us the opportunity to express our love for our fragile baby in song.

Alone At Home

Unaccountably, our rear tires found purchase on something—perhaps weeds and barley washed out by the flood—in the slippery mud. The car crawled slowly out of hub-deep water, tires churning in a muddy wake.

"Thank you," Mama sobbed.

In one hundred yards, we left the miry dirt road behind, and Mama drove faster on the gravel road that marked the Madison–Teton County line. Holly's breathing eased a bit. Soon we pulled up at Uncle Lester's shop, where Dad and Uncle Lester waited out the storm.

Dad ran to the car. As I tumbled out the passenger door, Mama slid across the front seat and took my place holding the oxygen tube for the thirty-nine winding miles to Ashton Memorial Hospital, where Holly had been born.

As I watched them go, I wondered if the doctors and nurses could help Holly. How long would we go down this road—not the terrifying road we'd just traveled, but the road we'd walked for the past four months—a road of constant worry about this tiniest member of our family?

***

Uncle Lester was a gentle giant, the quietest of my Nelson uncles. I told him I needed to get back to Andrea and Shanan, and he motioned me toward his pickup truck. Thankfully, the thunder and hail had stopped, but rain drummed down, and water streamed in low places. With four-wheel drive and a higher chassis, he deftly steered through and around mud holes that had frightened Mama and me. He showed me where the storm had ruined his barley crop.

As we walked into the house, Shanan ran to me, sobbing, "I wetted the bed!"

Andrea spluttered about the thunder and how she'd changed Shanan's clothes. The house was a mess, and I grabbed a dishrag to wipe the dish-cluttered table—a job Mama had asked me to do three hours before. My face burned. Uncle Lester's family was an orderly bunch.

In two strides, Uncle Lester crossed the room and scooped Shanan into his arms. "That's all right, honey. I had three little girls, and they all wet the bed sometimes. You girls come home with me. If there's more rain, you might be stranded."

"Thanks," I mumbled. Andrea ducked her head to hide her tear-stained face, and I put an arm around her as we walked to the truck.

Crowded into his pickup, we bumped along in a light drizzle. At his farmhouse, Uncle Lester poured milk and gave us gingersnaps made by Aunt Hazel, who was in Rexburg at their town home.

We'd only eaten a few when Bruce, Rex, and Lester's son, Theron, pulled up.

"Your folks are taking Holly to the Ashton hospital," Uncle Lester said.

Bruce said, "Yeah, we figured as much when we passed them on the highway. Finish your cookies, girls."

The sun shone, and things were a little drier as we went back through the puddles, with Bruce showing off his fanciest but slowest driving.

The house was empty, damp, and smelled of pee. I put Shanan in the bathtub to play while I stripped the bedsheets.

"I have to fill that dang washer and wash these!" I mumbled.

"D-Debbie?" Andrea was curled up on the couch, wiping her eyes with her arm.

"Hey, what's the matter?"

"I was so…so scared, Debbie. I know I'm a big girl, but the thunder was loud! I wish you never told me that thunder is giants throwing bowling balls down the mountain. Because our canyon is at the bottom of the mountain, and those giants might come here! After you left, blue lightning went across the corner of the kitchen. I ran to the bedroom and curled up next to Shanan on the bed."

My jaw fell. "I'm sorry, honey…"

"The worst was when Heavenly Father didn't answer my prayer," she sobbed. I handed her the toilet paper from the back of the couch. "I asked Him to please make the hail stop, and the thunder; to help Mama and Debbie get Daddy; that Holly can feel better, and that she won't have to have oxygen all the time; to help me take good care of Shanan. Then I felt something warm! That little twerp wet the bed. I was so mad I yelled!"

She blew her nose. "I'm still mad."

"Andi…*Andrea*, you did a good job. You were brave in the storm, and it stopped, just like you prayed! Guess what—your prayer helped Mama drive through the mud holes and not get stuck! We got Dad, and they're taking Holly to the doctor right now. Shanan's all right. There are worse things than wetting the bed."

"B-but here's the bad part. Holly is everything to Mama, and I can't do anything but sing to her. I can't hold her and keep that tube in the right place. Once Mama held both me and Holly and rocked us in the new chair. B-but sometimes, I wish she'd rock only me!" Andrea finished with a wail.

My tears fell on Andrea's curly hair. *I could not have*

faced the storm she faced alone—today, or ever. For a long time, I'd treated her so…so much like Bea treated me. I didn't know where the path of reconciliation started, but I went to the rocking chair and opened my arms. She climbed onto my lap.

"We can rock each other!" she laughed. We rocked that chair like crazy until Shanan ran naked into the room, then all three of us rocked and laughed.

***

After a while, Bruce called me into the kitchen where he stared dejectedly into the fridge. "Hey, Deb, got any ideas for supper?"

"All I know how to make is cookies. And biscuits."

"Touché." He grinned. "We're out of bread. Could you whip up some biscuits? I promise—no smart remarks. I'll fix scrambled eggs with leftover elk steak chopped up in it."

Bruce's eggs smelled good: a pinch of garlic powder was his secret ingredient. My biscuits seemed okay, spread with lots of Aunt Lola's rhubarb-strawberry jam, but nothing tasted good enough for us to eat much. The house felt empty, even after Uncle Ern dropped Brenda off at about nine.

When we heard the Fairlane coming at 10:11 p.m., Bruce, Brenda, Rex, Andrea, Shanan, and I crowded onto the front steps.

Dad and Mama didn't open the car's back door to get Holly. They left her bassinet and oxygen tank in the back seat. They climbed the terrace, blinded by the feeble beam of the porch light, looking shrunken, in darkness that was far too dense for a summer night.

Someone snapped this picture at the Teton–Newdale Cemetery, August 7, 1967. From left to right: Dad, Mama, me (on the ground), Ellen, Rex, Silver, Brenda, Kerry, and either Andrea or a cousin, gathered around Holly's grave.

The Comfort Of Truth

Mama said Holly's breathing got more labored the whole way, no matter what she tried. Dad drove as fast as he dared. Holly was alive when they carried her into the hospital, but soon, her butterfly breaths stilled.

Holly Joyce Nelson, and her Mama and Dad, beat the odds for 121 days, and each offered an acceptable sacrifice. The battle with her tiny, flawed body was over. Holly's glorious spirit was free.

***

Saturday, August 5, 1967

CLEMENTSVILLE

Dad and Mama dressed in their Sunday best and went to the funeral chapel. They called Judy and Jeanne from Teton and went to Rexburg to tell Ellen and Kerry, who didn't have a phone. Ellen had gotten Lance to sleep after a long night, and she wondered if she should put Lance into Mama's arms. She thought Mama might be hungry to hold a baby, but Ellen hated to wake him. The moment passed, and Dad and Mama left to tell our Grandma Nelson.

That night I wrote in my diary: ***Our Holly died yesterday. I cried a lot last night but somehow can't think of her as being dead. Maybe it is the assurance that she is with our Father in Heaven & with Grandma Rhodie. She was so quiet, and she suffered so much. Sweetly she came into the world and sweetly she left. Jeanne and Alan came, and we went to Rexburg and shopped. We had a lot of company. I hope the influence of her sweet life will stay with us the rest of our lives. Amen.***

***

Sunday, August 6, 1967

CLEMENTSVILLE

Dad stared at his hands, resting on a stack of bills. His coffee was cold, and he hadn't touched his oatmeal. Alan came into the kitchen, carrying scriptures. Brenda, doing dishes by my side, gave me a look. We quieted our hands and kept our backs to them. People seldom opened the Bible or Book of Mormon to Dad.

"Wayne, I...I thought it would be a comfort to you to know what the Book of Mormon teaches about infants who die." Alan's face was red up to his ears.

"All right." Dad was gruff.

"Holly is saved. She suffered in life, but now her spirit is with Jesus, and her physical problems ended when she died. Her body will be perfect when she's resurrected. You and Joyce will be able to raise her someday."

Alan opened his Book of Mormon. "The prophet Mormon said, 'Little children cannot repent; Wherefore, it is awful wickedness to deny the pure mercies of God unto them, for they are all alive in him because of his mercy.... For behold that all little children are alive in Christ...' That's Moroni 8:19 and 22. Alma wrote that after we die, our physical ailments will be healed, and we will someday 'be restored to our proper and perfect frame.' Holly's physical problems will be healed."

The red clock ticked loudly against the pink walls.

Dad grasped Alan's hand in a vice-grip handshake, then wiped his eyes and blew his nose into a red bandana.

Rex brought in the milk, and the kitchen got noisy.

Diary, Sunday, August 6, 1967: Somehow I don't mourn for Holly. All I can say is that I know she is safe and that she is in the celestial kingdom. Today I took care of the little girls. Everyone was going to the Memorial [funeral] Chapel but it rained and one carload couldn't go, me included.

***

Monday, August 7, 1967

TETON

I lifted Shanan up to look inside Holly's delicate white casket. Shanan asked, "Is this her bassinet now?"

Why do we look at Holly after she's dead? I want to remember what she was like when she was alive. She seemed tinier, and her color was not natural. She was dressed like a doll in a beautiful white satin dress made by Aunt Hazel and Aunt Nellie, and she wore white satin booties from Grandma Nelson. Holly's head was turned, with the pillow fluffed, so we couldn't see her rosebud ear, and her hair was in a "million-dollar hairdo." Shanan clung to my neck. I didn't want to put her down, so I carried her into the funeral.

Bishop Stewart did a good job conducting his first funeral. He cried a little. He was Grandma Rackham's nephew, and he had a good heart. Marilyn's sister Margie gave the life sketch, which Mama had been writing all weekend. Jeanne typed part of it, but Mama finished the last two pages, long-hand, in the car. Mama wrote how, when she was pregnant, the doctor thought she had a tumor—and how happy we were when it turned out to be a baby. Mama told of Holly's birth, and her first weeks in Utah, and how the doctors and nurses did everything they could for Holly. She told how Dad and we kids helped with Holly's care. She thanked friends and family who brought food and visited. She didn't say anything about what she'd done, except: "We did all we could for Holly."

"Holly stayed with us twice as long as the doctors said she could. She was living on the love of the home into which Heavenly Father had placed her. Through her we have learned how much Heavenly Father loves us and this choice spirit He sent. There isn't sorrow in knowing she has gone back to Him." It was a long history for a baby. Mama had a lot to say about her tenth child.

I looked at the painting at the front of the chapel. *I can imagine Holly in Jesus's arms instead of that toddler in a blue robe. He would heal her rosebud ear.*

Uncle Verl said Holly's spirit was happy. She was with Jesus Christ, and Grandpa Joe Nelson, and with Grandma Rhodie and Grandpa Will Furniss and their six children. Someday, in the resurrection, her body would be perfect. She would be one of the tall, lovely Nelson girls—with dark hair like Mama and blue eyes like Daddy.

After the service, we drove to the Teton–Newdale Cemetery and gathered around a freshly dug grave. I hated to think of Holly's body going into that hole. *The three babies that died after Grandma Rackham delivered them are buried here somewhere. Bea's brother is here. We will both have someone in this cemetery.* For a moment I felt close to Bea, and sorry for her.

Andrea tugged Brenda's sleeve and asked, "What are we doing?"

Brenda knelt and whispered, "Uncle Bud will dedicate Holly's grave."

"What's 'dedicate'?"

"Well, God gives us a blessing at both ends of our lives on earth. Remember that Dad said the missionaries gave Holly a name and a blessing? Now Uncle Bud will bless Holly's grave so her body can rest here until she's resurrected."

Uncle Bud said, "We ask Thee to bless this plot of ground to be safe from destructive forces. We set it apart as a place of rest for Holly's body and for the bodies of other family members who will be buried here, until their spirits and bodies reunite and they rise to greet us in the resurrection."

He said "other family members." I shivered and looked at my family standing with bowed heads. *I don't want anyone else to die. Grandma Rackham would say God decided when each of us would be born, and He will decide when we die. Dear God, please give us strength when others die.*

My stomach growled.

"Amen," rumbled Uncle Bud.

We raised our heads, and Bishop Stewart reminded us that Relief Society sisters had a delicious meal waiting for us at the church. That made it easier for me to leave, but Mama and Dad were slow to walk to the Fairlane.

At the church, Andrea and I filled our plates to overflowing and sat by Dad. Until the past few days, Dad tucked in with an appetite, but today he picked at his food. Shanan came near, and Dad said, "Come here, honey. You can have this nice roll and butter."

He took her on his lap, trying to feed her the roll, Jell-O, and bites of ham, but she snuggled tighter into his arms and patted his face.

Dad kissed her white-blond hair. "You're my precious girl."

She twisted her head to look him in the eyes. "Do I have to die, too?"

Dad groped for a paper napkin to wipe his eyes.

Andrea threw her arms around Dad and Shanan, and my tears fell—not far from the girls' bathroom where I had judged Dad harshly a few months before. I patted his hand, grateful for the odor of Camel cigarettes on his breath and his rough hand on Shanan's hair. I didn't want any other Dad, or any other family.

Timothy Hidalgo (left) and Lance Frazier (right) played with our yellow cat, Zander, and me in the summer of 1968 in Teton. Michael, Timothy, and Lance were the first of forty-four grandchildren in the Wayne and Joyce clan.

Seventh Grade

Wednesday, August 16, 1967

CLEMENTSVILLE

Every August was an agony of deadlines: finishing 4-H projects before the county fair; harvesting, canning, and freezing garden vegetables, fruit, chokecherries, and huckleberries for winter; and making or buying new school clothes for each child. Helping with Holly had interfered, but we had sorely procrastinated our 4-H projects: "Yeast Breads" for Brenda and "Child Care" for me.

When the house quieted at 10:30 p.m., Mama sat us at the kitchen table to work on the record books that we hadn't touched for eight weeks.

"So, Deb, do ya think I made bread on June 13th, 17th, 20th, and 23rd?" Brenda asked.

"Sure, why not? Let's say I tended kids on June 23rd, 24th, and 26th. And 27th, 28th, 29th, and 30th."

"According to this," Brenda added another date, "I made a lot of bread this summer! I have to make bread tomorrow—however many batches it takes to get a decent loaf to turn in with this book."

"Don't forget the salt this time," Mama gave Brenda a little smile—nothing like her old "before Holly smile." She leaned against the sink, scrubbing beets. "Debbie Day-O, get your diary, and see if you did tend kids all those days."

"Naah, Mama, it's easier to make it up."

She glanced at my book. "Look at those smudges! Find a decent eraser, and write more neatly. Pretend that each letter is a little person, and make him or her the prettiest they can be."

"Mama! Letters aren't 'pretty little people!' My hands don't know how."

"You can write better than that!" Mama's handwriting was a lovely cursive; mine was barely readable, and it ticked me off.

"I don't want to write better than that."

"Well, work on your babysitting kit."

I pulled it out. Jeanne had helped me cover an ice cream carton with red polka-dot cloth, and I was making a "quiet book" to go in it.

"Mama, I need yarn to make hair for the stupid doll in my stupid quiet book."

"Look in the junk drawer."

I rummaged in the drawer, crammed topsy-turvy with stuff.

"There's no yarn! That stupid doll won't have hair, and my stupid project will get a white ribbon! I can't close this stupid drawer! I hate 4-H—why did we have to take stupid 4-H this summer?" I spied a tangle of brown yarn in the back of the drawer and pulled it out, determined to braid it, glue it into the book, and go to bed.

"Mama, I need your help!"

Mama had slipped into her bedroom, where she held one of Holly's nightgowns to her face and breathed its scent. Holly's bassinet was full of clothes, medicines, and baby bottles, but it was so empty. Dad had moved the oxygen tank back to the shop, but it would take Mama a long time to put Holly's things away.

I threw my arms around her, and we sobbed. Mama teared up so easily that she never said, "Don't cry!" We were always free to weep.

Diary, Wednesday, August 16, 1967: Looked for cow all morning. Cleaned house. Aunt Saville and Carmen brought cow. Milked, etc. How can I say how empty it is? Worked on 4-H all day, all night. I have to ask for God's help constantly. Mama is so good.

***

Monday, August 21, 1967

CLEMENTSVILLE

Dad drove us kids—all but Shanan, who had taken to snuggling into Mama and Dad's double bed in the middle of the night—to catch the school bus on the main highway.

Brenda fixed her hair and make-up during the half hour trip to Teton, planning to look good in case any boys, short or tall, checked her out. Andrea chattered to Rex across from us. We were the only South Fremont School District students on the bus—the others attended Madison County schools. The districts worked things out, though—we would board a South Fremont bus at Teton Elementary.

Now I *had* to think about the unknowns of junior high school in great big St. Anthony (which had about a thousand residents, while Teton had 293). *No, 292, now that Holly has died. There'll be 131 students, not twenty-six. Will I make friends? Will Bea reign supreme, or will popular girls from St. Anthony ace her out? What if Bea mocks me? That would hurt, but there are worse hurts. Like losing Holly. It was hard to know how to help her, but it was easy to love her. Our prayer before she was born—that she would be healthy—was answered "no." Yet lots of prayers were answered. We prayed that Holly wouldn't suffer, and she is no longer suffering. I prayed that she wouldn't die when Mama and I were driving through the storm—and she didn't. After seeing her struggle in the car, I'm relieved, poor little one. I guess Heavenly Father sent the best answers to all the prayers.*

We passed the Teton Church where I had learned about eternal life from lessons and pictures. *Do I believe I'll see Holly again?* I thought of Mama mixing formula and washing diapers, giving enemas and rocking Holly. *Mama is kind of like Abraham. She sacrificed a lot for Holly and in the end, she gave her back to God. Mama taught us by the things she did that Jesus loves Holly, and each of us, as much as Mama does.*

The engine of a combine growled outside, where a farmer was cutting wheat. *Dad and Mama gathered in many crops; Dad says kids are their greatest crop. Now they have returned a tenth of their harvest to God. He is watching over Holly now. It will take a long time, but we will be with her for eternity.*

We clambered off the bus at the red brick elementary school. *Oh no, where's Andrea? Is she okay? I won't be at the grade school to help her.* She elbowed me and said, "Good luck at your new school!"

I hugged her. "Good luck in second grade!"

Rowdy boys and popular girls sat in the back of the bus to the junior and senior high schools. Normal people like Brenda, Rex, and their friends sat in the middle.

People who found vague protection from being close to the back of the bus driver's head sat near the front. I slid into the second seat.

Bill pulled himself up the bus steps with his powerful arms, giggling about his crutches and jerky gait. Since his knees didn't bend, he let himself fall into the front seat with a bang. A kid from our class teased, "The school district is going to send you a bill for that!" Bill guffawed, and we joined him.

Other boys got on. Not one of them called me "De-bra." *They act better now that they are the youngest kids in junior high instead of the oldest in elementary school.*

Sandy waved at me, and I smiled at her. Bea got on, in all the glory of a new outfit from J.C. Penney, and murmured, "Sorry about your sister." She reached the back of the bus before I could catch my breath. *A smile from Sandy? Kindness from Bea? It may not last but I'll take it!*

Wendy leaned toward me, her face bright red, and handed me a note, then sat by herself and stared out the window. The crumpled paper read, "Dear Debra, I feel so bad about the way I treated you last year." *Oh, Wendy—were you my friend all along, and just too afraid to stand up to Bea?*

Our class had attended school together since first grade. Now we rolled out of Teton toward our future. Toward many new students—many new friends.

It had been a good summer on the farm. Difficult,

but good. *What will I remember? The hail, thunder, and lightning that taught me where to turn for safety? The songs of a thousand birds at daybreak, the millions of stars that burned in the sky? The chislers, wheeling hawks, grasshoppers, and covey of quail?*

I want to hang onto all of it.

Holly's last long look into my eyes on the day she died.

Waking and sleeping, I have treasured that gift for the rest of my life.

Two Precious Letters

Dr. Lechelt heard of Holly's death and wrote Mama and Dad a letter.

LETTERHEAD: Medical Center for Women and Children

August 17, 1967, Idaho Falls
Ninth at Oxford
Idaho Falls, Idaho

Mr. and Mrs. F. W. Nelson
Star Route
Newdale, Idaho

Dear Mr. and Mrs. Nelson:

Enclosed are the articles that you sent to me. I was

saddened to learn of Holly's death, but I'm sure that this was for the best.

Having read your letter, and meeting the two of you, I know that your lives were truly blessed by the experience of loving and caring for Holly. It gave me a real feeling of humility to read your letter and to realize how appreciative that you were of this opportunity to minister to this infant, and never once express a thought of futility or distress at the prospect. I'll long remember Holly, and her parents, and feel myself richer for the chance to know all of you, and to have been of some slight help during this period.

I am returning the articles that you had sent to me. Actually, I think that your letter is an even more telling inspirational story in its own way than are these articles. I think that it could be of help to other families who must face this problem, and have thought that maybe it should be published in some magazine, as it was written, with a brief explanatory note about your baby, and her subsequent course.

I would appreciate it if you would consider letting me send it in, and if so, to send me permission to do this. Naturally, if this was done, the names of you and Holly, as well as the hospital, and the physicians involved in her treatment would be changed. If any remuneration was forthcoming, this would be, in turn, forwarded to you to use as you see fit, but I would think possibly it could be given to the Primary Children's Hospital for the care of other children, or to some research organization, to further study newborn anomalies.

Thank you again for allowing me to help in caring for Holly.

Sincerely,

(signed)

Ronald K. Lechelt M.D.
RKL/gb

Enclosures [These have been lost]

Having read your letter, and meeting the two of you, I know that your lives were truly blest by the experience of loving and caring for Holly. It gave me a real feeling of humility to read your letter and to realize how appreciative that you were of this opportunity to minister to this infant, and never once express a thought of futility or distress at the prospect. I'll long remember Holly, and her parents, and feel myself richer for the chance to know all of you, and to have been of some slight help during this period.

I am returning the articles that you had sent to me. Actually, I think that your letter is an even more telling inspirational story in it's own way than are these articles. I think that it could be of help to other families who must face this problem, and have thought that maybe it should be published in some magazine, as it was written, with a brief explanatory note about your baby, and her subsequent course.

Dr. Lechelt sent this warm, validating letter to Mama and Dad shortly after Holly died. He wished to share Mama's methods with other parents, which would have been a blessing.

Writing a reply to Dr. Lechelt's letter must have been therapeutic for Mama. Here is her reply.

Undated (sometime after August 1967)

Mr. and Mrs. F. W. Nelson, Star Route, Newdale, Idaho

Dr. Ronald K. Lechelt
Pediatrician
Ninth at Oxford
Idaho Falls, Idaho

Dear Doctor,

Thank you sincerely for this letter. It's easy to understand why you chose to devote your life to the care of children—you have such a deep insight into the worth of every child.

We'd like to explain if we can, why we have hesitated to answer such a kind and considerate letter.

We were glad that, in your estimation we had written something that may help others. It was written in a time of stress, so that now it is hard to remember exactly what we said, but this I know, because we so desperately needed your help, we were completely honest with you. This is what troubles us now. After a serious discussion between my husband and I we decided to withhold a part of the tragic truth of Holly's condition from our children. This was the fact that there was a chromosome deficiency. Those two words carry such a dire meeting for me now that it leaves me trembling just to write them. Holly was about 18 days old when we were told that the tests had been returned, and she had a chromosome deficiency.

From the very time her Daddy left the Falls with her, after you had explained the results of your findings, we had known that she probably could not live. Dr. Veasy had explained that in her case there could be no operation, that her heart crowded her left lung, they had even told us of the probable damage to her liver, kidneys, and other organs. No one who examined her seemed to believe she could live more than just a few days. For us, our children, their dear grandmother, and others, this was sufficient, we were prepared to love her while we could and accept her going as God's will.

I must try to explain the reasons we brought forth, in that lonely motel room, for not telling our family this added sadness. Four of our children are grown. They've been to college and in the service, three of them are married. Our two oldest daughters were expecting babies, one in May, one in June; we wished to spare them undue worry and anxiety about the lives growing within them, to let the coming of their babies be as happy an experience as possible. (The oldest, a registered nurse, searching through her books, had hit upon an answer of sorts, as to what may have caused Holly's troubles: "Defects to the unborn child may result from undetermined illnesses of the mother such as diabetes, thyroid disturbances, high blood pressure, acute or chronic or recurrent kidney infections." Even as a girl I had kidney infections. In the sixth month of pregnancy with the child next older than Holly, I was hospitalized with a kidney infection, However, she was a very healthy baby, as were all the others. A year ago, in September I was in Rexburg, caring for my husband's mother when I became quite ill. Our family doctor is in Ashton, but I decided on one of the Rexburg doctors; he examined me and said it was not a pregnancy, but a tumor, and advised a specialist in Idaho Falls. I went to him and he scheduled an operation. When I went down to be entered in the hospital, they discovered that the tumor was a child! Everyone was happy! Dr. Melcher in Ashton said there had probably been some kidney infection, which had cleared up with the medication the Rexburg doctor had given me.

The same book in which our daughter found this information offered another explanation that perhaps could have been the reason for Holly's illness. (During the fifth month of my pregnancy with her, our younger children had German measles. Our doctor assured us that I was far enough along that the unborn child could not be harmed.) Now, however, the book said, "The rubella virus which causes German measles, it has now been determined, can cause defects at any time during pregnancy, i.e., malformations of the heart, deafness, blindness, mental retardation – either singly or in any combination; during a recent German measles epidemic, many women who were definitely exposed to the disease were never ill; therefore both the patient and the physician were of the opinion that the patient had not had rubella, yet some of these women gave birth to infants with characteristic malformations. Research indicates that the chances of having a defective child, should rubella occur, vary from 10 to 20%. To date no satisfactory method for the prevention of rubella following exposure is available, since the virus is now recognized, it is hoped that a vaccine like that for polio and measles will soon be available."

Doctor, perhaps we are wrong, but my husband and I thought that neither of these circumstances could have caused a chromosome deficiency. Do you know if that is the case? Also, could you tell us if the tendency to have chromosome deficient children could be inherited by our children? This was our really big reason for not telling our family all the doctor had told us. If there is any chance of this, we would rather they not have this ominous worry hanging over them through all the years they are getting their families; particularly since there seems to be so little known about the causes. We plan to learn as much as we can on this subject, then if there comes a time when it would be better if any or all of them knew that Holly died from a chromosome deficiency rather than an enlarged heart, we will tell them.

One more thing I feel I should mention—there remains with us just the smallest shadow of doubt that she had chromosome deficiency. When we asked the doctor if the chromosome tests had come back, he answered us with these words: "Oh, well, we are certain that is her trouble." Because of the fact that we had nine other children who had been born with no defects, and that there is no history of defects on either side, we did not think it was "hiding our heads under a bushel" or dodging the truth or anything, to believe that the kidney ailments which I have always had, or the German measles, could have been the cause. At that time, our baby and what was to be done to help her were what mattered, far more than what may have caused her condition. Now, however, since we can never have another child, we are anxious to do only that which is best for our other children and grandchildren.

Doctor, if the letter we wrote could still help others—if the dreaded words "chromosome deficiency" were omitted, and it was just mentioned that there was no hope for her because of the enlarged heart which in her case could not be operated upon, then we would appreciate very much having you send it in. I'm sure, though, that you'd better ask your secretary or someone who can type much better than I, to retype it.

Thank you for your kindness and friendship.

Sincerely, Mrs. Joyce Nelson
Star Route

Newdale, Idaho

Just a little added note. We felt that when you learned of Holly's death, you would be concerned that we may have withheld the oxygen from her, we hadn't. She surely rallied the last few days and we were all were so encouraged and enjoyed her so much, but did not change her oxygen or medicine or anything. However, the day we lost her, there came a terrible hailstorm, this terrified her, she cried and fought for air—we could not give her enough oxygen to help, it seemed. Our 12-year-old prepared the oxygen in the car and we placed the baby in her bassinet with the oxygen on her and drove toward Ashton. In places the water and hail were hub-deep – but just as He had been all the while we had her, God was only just a prayer away. We stopped at Wayne's brother's place just long enough to get Wayne. (His brother took our 12-year-old back to our place to stay with the two younger children.) Wayne drove and I worked with the baby, trying somehow to help her breathe. At the hospital they worked every way they knew, but they could not save her. The Ashton doctors said that the lower atmospheric conditions made it harder for her to breathe. Wayne and I were grateful we did not lose her at home, for the little kids who loved her so were there, and we were very glad we were both with her.

Doctor, the little grandchildren we were expecting in May and June were just perfect! Both boys, one born on Mother's Day and one the day after the Fourth of July.

One more thing, because I know you're busy, but doctor if you ever know of a baby who needs a home, could you let us know? We don't know the first thing about adopting a child and we haven't an abundance of money, and we're probably too old, but one thing we have plenty of around here is love.

Thanks again for everything.

Sincerely,
Joyce Nelson

Enclosure: permission form

We give, Dr. Ronald K. Lechelt M.D. our permission to send in for publication:

("A letter written to him,-by us-, at a time when our baby was desperately ill.")

with the sincere hope that it may help others facing a similiar problem.

In the event that it is published, and any renumeration is forthcoming we wish this to go to the L.D.S. Primary Children's Hospital, Salt Lake City, Utah for the care of other critically ill babies.

Sincerely,

Mr. & Mrs. F. Wayne Nelson
Star Route,
Newdale, Idaho

F. Wayne Nelson
Joyce Furniss Nelson

Mama and Dad were willing to have Mama's letter printed, and to give monetary proceeds to the Primary Children's Hospital.

Since 1977, Wayne and Joyce's progeny have gathered for a reunion close to Wayne's birthday on July 7. Since 1987, we've had a camping reunion at the farm. This photo was taken in the farmhouse living room around 1997. From left to right: (Back) Rex, Judy, Bruce, Shanan, Debbie; (Front) Brenda, Ellen, Mama, Jeanne; Andrea in front of Mama. We've remained close over the years, bound tightly together by the love of our parents, our Savior Jesus Christ, and our sister—Holy Holly.

What Happened Afterward

During the fall of 1967, we moved slowly from the farm—one carload at a time, into November. Mama didn't want to leave, perhaps sensing that we wouldn't spend another summer there. She didn't take the Christmas tree down until Valentine's Day. Mama grieved and suffered from depression, but she didn't quit living, loving, and sacrificing. She took her children and grandchildren to church and encouraged them to walk in the March of Dimes Walkathon, which supported research into birth defects.

Dad attended church often that winter. I wrote in my diary, close to my thirteenth birthday: "*Monday, February 5, 1968: Cleaned the house before missionaries came. They will have Dad converted; I think. I'm so happy.... Tuesday,*

February 6: Patches died today. Dad really fixed him nice." Teton didn't have leash laws, and dogs roamed free. Perhaps a farmer was annoyed when dogs harassed his livestock—in any case, curious Patches was the one to find the poisoned meat. We were devastated. Dad led us in a funeral; he even said the prayer. I didn't know he was also trying to quit smoking. His interest in religion waned when bugging season began, and 1968 was one of our best bugging years.

When the Forest Service ended its pine beetle spraying initiative a few years later, Dad bid on Bureau of Land Management fence building jobs in the desert. He also worked as a ditch rider on the Teton–Newdale Canal, and for twelve years as a night watchman at the Idaho Stud Mill.

Dad and I took the camper bus to the Idaho desert three weeks before my marriage to Norman Holm in the Idaho Falls Temple in 1976. Herds of antelope kept their distance, as if they knew we were licensed and ready to shoot them. We never connected, but we savored the precious time together.

Dad and Mama encouraged their children to graduate from college. As we grew up, married and left home, we scattered geographically. Dad was baptized and confirmed a member of The Church of Jesus Christ of Latter-day Saints on December 1, 1984, about the time their nest emptied. He died in 1989.

We all wept tears of joy, and Mama was thrilled, when Dad's brother Lester served as proxy for Wayne, and

Wayne, Joyce, and nine of their children were sealed together in the Logan Temple of The Church of Jesus Christ of Latter-day Saints. Their oldest granddaughter, Rebekah Jeppesen, served as proxy for Holly as we surrounded the altar dressed in white, as Mama had envisioned.

Many people say ten children is too many—during the 1960s, now, or any time. Yet Dad and Mama felt their family was just right: every flawed and faulty one of us was a priceless treasure. They welcomed their children's spouses in the same spirit, and lavished time and love on their grandchildren. The following children, in-law children, and grandchildren loved Grandpa Nelson and honored Joyce by calling her "Grammy":

Judy and Silver Hidalgo: Michael, Timothy, Daniel, and Anita Hidalgo (after Judy and Silver divorced, she married Glenn Scoble)

Bruce and Janice (Wakley) Nelson (divorced about 2001): Nicholaus and Mariel Nelson

Ellen and Kerry Frazier: Lance, Jennifer, Patricia, Derrick, Shane, and Aaron Frazier

Jeanne and Alan Jeppesen: Rebekah, Amelia, Kevin, Erik, and Kristen Jeppesen

Brenda and Shae Anderson: Ann Marie, Nathan, Yvonne "Vonnie", Bryan, Alison, Owen, Meggan, Evan, Brett, Rachael, and Robert Anderson

Rex and Sulin (Reid) Nelson: Nicolette, Nisha, Wayne, Bryce, and Isaac Nelson

Debbie and Norman Holm: Lara, Janson, Emily, Spencer, and Alissa Holm

Andrea and Ross Clark: Joseph, Matthew, Hyrum, and Beth Clark

Shanan and Kelly Cameron (divorced in 2020): Adam and Joshua Cameron

Vonnie Anderson, a favorite sibling, cousin, and niece, has Down Syndrome. Her happy smile and warm heart radiate at the center of our family's love.

Brenda carried heavy burdens. She and Shae lost two sons at early ages. Owen died of Sudden Infant Death Syndrome in 1982, and Brett died in an accidental drowning in 1990. Both were buried near Holly. Mama died in 2009. We decorate five graves in the Teton–Newdale Cemetery on Memorial Day. Brenda's and Andrea's families moved to Ohio, where Brenda died in 2000 of complications from leukemia. Andrea's son Hyrum died in 2002 in a car accident caused by a drunk driver. Our family decorates two graves in Ohio.

The farm isn't deserted. Since 1987, our ever-growing families have gathered near Wayne's July birthday for a camping reunion. Soon, our parents' great-great grandchildren will join the happy throngs who swing, run down the dugway, and explore the canyon. Family members visit at other times of year as well. To many people, it's a dusty, waterless environment, but to us, it is decidedly heaven. I believe that Holly's influence is the key to our family unity and inspires the magic of our family reunions.

Epilogue

You don't have to die to see your life pass before your eyes.

I learned that in an airplane in 2007 above Idaho's Upper Snake River Valley. My skin tingled, telling me that places below should be familiar. I struggled for perspective, for I was high in the air and farther north than the roads I'd always traveled.

At last, I recognized a patch of green on a hillside. Under that distant grass rested the bodies of my sister, father, and two nephews. Everything inside me reached for that place, and for my rapidly passing childhood homes: the gray stone house in Teton, and twenty miles east, a home in a canyon that creases the skirts of the Big Hole Mountains.

On its relentless eastward arc, the plane approached the Teton Range, flying nonchalantly over places that made me weep for joy and twisted my heart with pain. Why did they wrench me to the core? I had moved away from these homes thirty years before. Wasn't it time that I "got over it?"

My mother would understand my up-in-the-air emotions. At age eighty-seven, Mama's heart was in those homes. She and Dad raised nine fine children, yet it was the tenth child, sleeping in that cemetery, that tied her to the place most profoundly.

When Holly was sent home with congenital birth defects, Mama devoted herself to her care. Mama had poured herself into all her children, from ironing clothes in the morning to listening to dating troubles at midnight. She nurtured us through illnesses and injuries and gave frequent, tight hugs. She loved her family fiercely—if she loved Holly, or any of us too well, it was because she chose love over any easier option. She loved Dad even more deeply than she loved her children, and he loved her in the same way.

Smart, witty, and physically strong, Dad lived after the time when a hardworking dry farmer could make a decent living for his family on a smaller acreage, and smack dab in the time when the same farmer needed either more land and equipment, or a job that required a college education, to keep his family afloat. Lacking those advantages, he thrust his hands between his family and poverty. I touched Dad's right hand—large-knuckled, calloused, scarred, with a fingernail painted bright red because the nail was splitting and he liked bright colors—on the day we buried him in 1989. Those hands held babies, caressed little heads, baited fishhooks, welded car parts, gestured a story's punchline, and worked, and worked, and worked. Dad wore his hands out giving love.

As the plane bounced into boiling clouds, I thought of our family's graves. The first of those graves, dug for the tiniest body, wrung my heart. Holly brought Mama and Dad to the doorway of the furnace of their greatest affliction, where they turned their faces to the flames and stepped in.

* * *

NOTES

I wanted to tell Holly's story for many years. After Brenda died, her daughter found my ragtag diary in her mother's things and sent it to me. I excitedly deciphered the scrawled entries and typed it, but when I showed the typescript to Mama in 2007, she was wounded by the casual way her twelve-year-old daughter had interpreted events that so consumed her. I had written about all aspects of our lives; her life had centered on Holly. Though Mama was a prolific writer, she was unable to write about Holly beyond her letters to Dr. Lechelt and the life story she wrote during the thirty-six hours after Holly died, nor could she bear the thought of anyone else probing her personal Gethsemane. I set the story aside in deference to her feelings. Mama died on December 31, 2009.

An unexpected miracle in 2016 brought a new perspective to Holly's story. Dr. Ronald Lechelt had been retired for several years when he found letters pertaining to Holly in his desk. Knowing only that the Nelson family he had helped fifty years before lived somewhere near Rexburg, he started calling Nelson names in telephone directory. Luckily, our cousin Albert Nelson was one of the first entries, and Albert's wife Joan had Dr. Lechelt mail the letters to her. Joan passed them on to Ellen. I interviewed Dr. Lechelt in person in 2017. He was very kind, and said that gentle touching and listening are two of a doctor's greatest tools. With his help, I was able to interview Dr. George Veasy by telephone. Despite diligent research, I could not obtain hospital records from the hospitals where Holly was treated or get contact information for other doctors. (Dr. Willis Melcher, our family physician, died almost exactly a year after Holly was born.) I had a delightful interview with my sixth-grade teacher, Gerald Gee.

With these sources I should have whipped out the memoir in record time, yet even after Mama was gone, I battled a hidden psychological demon—my *inner child.* She didn't want me to share our family's tender, personal, painful story. Writer's block and my penchant for putting other writing projects and life demands ahead of the memoir slowed me down. It also seemed that God had a timetable for this book, just as He has a timetable for the development and birth of a baby. I had to follow His rhythm. Finally, I asked this child's permission to share our story, promising that we would both be okay if I did. We persevered, and this book is the result.

With love, faith in God, support from medical practitioners, and family resiliency, there's hope at the end of every rainbow—like this one at the Nelson Farm during our reunion in 2008.

Appendix A

When I visited with Dr. Lechelt in 2017, he told me Holly's condition was perhaps a syndrome. Nowadays, doctors would have a name for that syndrome, and they could do more to treat a child such as Holly, but they didn't have the necessary tests and medical innovations in 1967.

Holly wasn't the only member of our family treated at Primary Children's Hospital. Jeanne and Alan's son, Kevin, underwent two minor surgeries there and their son, Erik, underwent neurosurgery on the front suture of his skull at three months of age. Mama sat with Jeanne at Primary Children's during that time. Jeanne wrote, "I feel grateful that when we needed it, we lived close to the best hospital for children in the intermountain West."

Among Nelson grandchildren and great-grandchildren, medical teams in many cities have treated a brain tumor, a cleft palate, meningitis, a heart defect, and several premature births. Nurses and doctors have displayed utmost compassion to our family, and we extend heartfelt thanks to all dedicated medical professionals.

In 2014, my three-year-old grandson was diagnosed with acute promyelocytic leukemia (APL). This cancer is rare in children but has more successful treatment outcomes than other leukemias. After reading Mom's and Dr. Lechelt's letters, my daughter, Lara Joyce Holm Roetto, wrote this email to her son's oncologist. It expresses our family's gratitude for miracles, modern medicine, and caring professionals.

Jan. 19, 2017

Dear Dr. (name omitted for privacy),

Last week I received a copy of letters my Grandmother had written to her sick infant's pediatrician 50 years ago. Her sweet baby had a heart condition and wasn't expected to live. Sadly, the baby died shortly after my grandmother wrote to him. Her words to him were so heartfelt. It was full of gratitude to this young doctor, earnest questions about her baby's condition, and advice for him to pass on to other parents who may be going through a similar situation. Fifty years later, this retired doctor still had this letter and another from her, and he sought out my Grandma's children to give them copies.

Reading her letters made me realize I should do the same for you. So here goes…

Hands down the worst day of our lives was when our boy was admitted into the hospital with leukemia. It was excruciating. Our hearts were broken and we were so so scared. I don't think it was chance that you were in the hospital that day. Your approach was just what we needed. I'll never forget you saying, "It's totally treatable." In that instant, so much worry melted away. As long as it was treatable, no matter what the odds, I felt comfort that he would be okay.

I remember you coming into our room after looking at his blood for hours trying to figure out what type of leukemia he had. You looked so tired. I remember our world being shaken as you told us it definitely wasn't ALL, most likely AML, or a very small chance it was APL. I remember asking you to go with us into a different room as I broke down. The heaviness of AML and its treatment loomed over us. The chance of losing our son made me despondent.

I'm sure as an oncologist you have learned to guard your heart somewhat. You've probably had to give a lot of really bad news to many wonderful people.

On the flip side, we as parents of sick kids don't guard our hearts to you. Instead, we reach to you in hope. We look to you as the one who will be able to save our kid, to do for them what we can't. We revere you. We honor and reverence your knowledge.

The next day when you came to tell us that he definitely had APL, I felt your earnest happiness for us! It still touches me how happy we were to get such awful news from you!

You've seen us through these years of treatment with support and kindness. You always had a smile and a great attitude. I remember a slow day at the clinic when you sat down and played a game with my son and me. We have always felt he was safe in your hands. Thanks to your knowledge and guidance, he is flourishing!

There really is no way to thank you for all you've done for us. It may be easy for you to think that if it wasn't you it would have been some other doctor. But my point in writing this is to tell you that YOU matter to us. You had the unique personality and calm disposition to help us walk through this hellish situation with optimism and hope. We are so grateful for you. Thank you.

Lara Roetto

P.S. You don't have to hang onto this for 50 years ;)

The doctor replied:

Wow! This is truly one of the nicest things any patient (or family) has ever done. Thank you so much.

Perhaps the biggest thing that drew me to medicine initially was an experience I had where I witnessed the power a physician can have beyond medicine to affect the lives of patients and families – for better or worse. That experience gave me a desire to be in a position where I could have that influence, and I hoped that I would be the kind of person that could make a positive impact.

Thus, your kind words are particularly validating for me. Thank you, again.

Also, congratulations on the bone marrow result. It was no great surprise, but it is still so nice to see it in writing, so to speak.

Let's keep this thing permanently in our rear-view mirror!!!

Appendix B

Text of 2016 Handwritten Letter from Dr. Ronald K. Lechelt

19 Nov. 2016

To the family of Wayne and Joyce Nelson,

*I do not believe I ever met Joyce, as Holly was brought to the Idaho Falls hospital at a few hours of age and then taken to Salt Lake City.**

However, when I found these letters from Joyce, I knew that she was a very loving, caring mother. As you will see in the letters, she did not want her children and their spouses to worry about any genetic familial concerns.

Now chromosome studies, as well as other tests, probably would have identified a specific diagnosis for Holly, but in 1967 these tests were not yet known.

When I found this letter in the corner of my desk, I re-read it, and I knew that her family had to read it—even if she did not want you to worry at that time. I hope you do not think I am not honoring her wishes at that time. However, I think that at this time, this will help you to know and love her even more and to realize how much she loved all of you.

Sincerely,

Ronald (Ron) K. Lechelt, M.D.

*I recorded in my diary on August 1, 1967: *"Mama and Dad took Holly to Dr. Lashell [sic]. She weighs seven pounds and six ounces and is doing well. Played around and read." Perhaps they took her to a different doctor, and I wrote the wrong name. Or, it would not be unusual for Dr. Lechelt, as a busy pediatrician, to have forgotten the visit of a one-time patient in his office, especially after nearly fifty years.*

Bibliography

Letters in the possession of Debra Nelson Holm:

1. From Joyce Nelson to Dr. Ronald K. Lechelt July 14, 1967
2. From Dr. Ronald Lechelt to Joyce and Wayne Nelson, August 17, 1967
3. From Joyce and Wayne Nelson to Dr. Lechelt (Undated, after August of 1967)
4. From Joyce Nelson to Judy Hidalgo May 1967
5. From Wayne Nelson to Judy Hidalgo May 1967

Interviews with family members, mostly from 2007-2022; Notes in the possession of Debra Nelson Holm. Bruce Nelson was especially helpful with details about bugging.

Interview with Dr. Ronald K. Lechelt, September 16, 2017 at his home. Notes in the possession of Debra Nelson Holm.

Interview with George Veasy MD, September 29, 2017 by telephone. Notes in the possession of Debra Nelson Holm.

Rex Nelson "How to Spray a Bug Tree," unpublished essay, 1971, in the possession of Debra Nelson Holm.

Bob Liang "Agony of mothers about their unborn: 20,000 babies will be damaged by nationwide epidemic" *LIFE* June 4, 1965, https://books.google.com/books?id=8VIEAAAAMBAJ&pg=PA3&source=gbs_toc_r&cad=2#v=onepage&q&f=false.

D. A. Leatherman "Trees and Shrubs. Mountain Pine Beetle," https://static.colostate.edu/client-files/csfs/pdfs/MPB.pdf https://csfs.colostate.edu/forest-management/common-forest-insects-diseases/mountain-pine-beetle/.

S. A. Mata, J. M. Schmid, D. A. Leatherman "Diesel Fuel Oil for increasing mountain pine beetle mortality in felled logs," 2002 https://www.fs.usda.gov/treesearch/pubs/28867.

"Big Two-Hearted River, Item: Public Domain, https://www.wikidata.org/wiki/Q3775616.